CAPITAL CAMPAIGNERS

SUBADAR-MAJOR MIR KAMBIR KHAN
A Baluch Indian Officer, 1919

CAPITAL CAMPAIGNERS

The History of the 3rd Battalion
(Queen Mary's Own)
The Baluch Regiment

by
LIEUTENANT-COLONEL W. E. MAXWELL, C.I.E.

The Naval & Military Press Ltd

Reproduced by kind permission of the Central Library,
Royal Military Academy, Sandhurst

Published by
The Naval & Military Press Ltd
Unit 10, Ridgewood Industrial Park,
Uckfield, East Sussex,
TN22 5QE England
Tel: +44 (0) 1825 749494
Fax: +44 (0) 1825 765701
www.naval-military-press.com
www.military-genealogy.com

© The Naval & Military Press Ltd 2007

The Naval & Military Press ...

...offer specialist books for the serious student of conflict. The range of titles stocked covers the whole spectrum of military history with titles on uniforms, battles, official histories, specialist works containing Medal Rolls and Casualties Lists, and numismatic titles for medal collectors and researchers.

The innovative approach they have to military bookselling and their commitment to publishing have made them Britain's leading independent military bookseller.

In reprinting in facsimile from the original, any imperfections are inevitably reproduced and the quality may fall short of modern type and cartographic standards.

DEDICATED

TO

THE MEMORY OF ALL RANKS

3RD BATTALION (QUEEN MARY'S OWN) THE BALUCH REGIMENT

WHO DIED IN WAR

CONTENTS

			Page
CHAPTER ONE	1844—1856	. . . . . .	1
CHAPTER TWO	1856—1866	. . . . . .	11
CHAPTER THREE	1867—1889	. . . . . .	25
CHAPTER FOUR	1889—1908	. . . . . .	34
CHAPTER FIVE	1908—1914	. . . . . .	43
CHAPTER SIX	1914—1918	. . . . . .	55
CHAPTER SEVEN	1918—1929	. . . . . .	68
CHAPTER EIGHT	1929—1940	. . . . . .	80
CHAPTER NINE	July, 1941—June, 1942	. . . .	91
CHAPTER TEN	June, 1942—August, 1943	. . . .	115
CHAPTER ELEVEN	Italy, 1943—1944	. . . . .	132
CHAPTER TWELVE	Greece, 1944—1946	. . . .	146
APPENDIX I.—List of Commanding Officers		. . . .	160
APPENDIX II.—Bibliography	. . . . . .		161
INDEX	. . . .		163

PLATES

SUBADAR-MAJOR MIR KAMBIR KHAN	. *Frontispiece*
	Facing Page
The Original Colours of 1st Belooch	18
The Abyssinian Christian Cross	28
Regimental Types	74
The Officers, 1924	76
Colonel A. C. Taylor, D.S.O.	134
The Officers, 1946	156

MAPS

Campaigns, 1844—1939	Front End Paper
East Africa	67
Sicily and Italy	145
Campaigns, 1941—1946	Back End Paper

CHAPTER ONE

1844—1856

THE policy of Sir Charles Napier which resulted in the conquest of Sind and its annexation to the British Empire in India after a campaign which may be termed smart, in both a political and military sense, has not received the commendation of moralists. It had, however, many fortunate and beneficial results for India: and not least among these was the formation of those Baluch regiments which have attained so honoured a place in the annals of the Indian Army.

All opposition to the forces of Sir Charles Napier had ceased by June of the year 1843, and the province as a whole had willingly accepted the change of rulers, accompanied as it obviously was by many material advantages. The Conqueror (as Sir Charles was invariably termed) preferred nevertheless to keep his government on a purely military basis in all branches of its administration. He succeeded in retaining a very large military force of some fifteen thousand men, partly because of the war with the Punjab, which was generally regarded as inevitable, and partly because he professed to regard invasion from Baluchistan and Afghanistan as a probable danger. It is hardly surprising, therefore, that he regarded the people of Sind, whose physique was so superior to that of the average Indian peasant, as likely to supply a good class of recruit for his army.

The first object was, to quote from the minute of Sir George Clerk, Governor of Bombay, dated the 24th of April, 1848, "to take up the loose soldiery of the country." It is true that, as John Jacob was ready to point out, there was no "loose soldiery," in the strict sense of the term, to be taken up. The Talpur Ameers defeated by Napier had employed no soldiers except a few hundred miscellaneous followers. Their armies had consisted of the followers and clansmen of the Baluch chieftains and landholders, who had answered the call to arms and had fought bravely if unskilfully at Meeanee and Hyderabad. "Braver barbarians," writes Napier after Meeanee, "never gave themselves to slaughter." When the Ameers had been overthrown and the landholders had readily submitted to the new regime, their followers had gone back to their cultivation. There was, nevertheless, a considerable floating population of persons without employment, largely consisting of men from the North, or beyond the border, whom it was well worth while to employ. There was, moreover, according to Sir George Clerk, the further object of rendering the British service attractive to the military classes in Sind. It must be remembered that at this time service in Sind was intensely unpopular with the Bengal Army sepoys who had been called on to garrison the upper portion of the province. The Bombay regiments had shown no such mutinous spirit, but they were few in numbers, and had difficulties of recruitment. Moreover, the calls on the expanding Indian Army as a whole were becoming increasingly heavy, and obviously too much reliance was being placed on the single great recruiting area of Oudh and the then North-West Provinces, from which the whole of the Bengal and a portion of the Bombay Armies were supplied. It is not surprising therefore that new areas were sought for, and that Napier desired to enrol the inhabitants of the province. In his proclamation of the 8th of May, 1844, it was announced that "Belooch and Sindee soldiers are required by His Excellency the Governor."

These classes were, however, not entirely new to military service. "Scindy" people had regularly been enrolled in the Bombay Army nearly a hundred years before, though in independent companies without any large degree of discipline. For many years they held a high reputation as mercenary soldiers in many parts of India, and were so employed in the Kathiawar States until a comparatively recent date. This may surprise those who know of the low estimate of the courage of the Sindhi held by the Baluchis, and indeed by the European officer, in modern times. Several reasons can, however, be given for this poor opinion. The Sindhi mercenaries, who had a high reputation outside Sind, probably came almost entirely from the predatory tribes such as the Numrias and Jokias, who occupied the hillier portions of Lower Sind. The mass of the agricultural and pastoral tribes had never, in all probability, any inclination for warfare. All the Sindhis, moreover, had been bullied and despised by the Baluchis, who, though they had been entering Sind for some centuries, had been in control of the country for only some sixty years before Napier's infiltration. These had always been warlike, but they had adopted the habits and language of the Sindhi inhabitants of the province they had overrun, and were already very different in manners and appearance from their relatives who had remained in Baluchistan. Napier, however, who had seen and admired the courage of his ill-disciplined and ill-armed opponents at the battles of the conquest, could not be expected to distinguish too closely between the Baluch and the Sindhi.

The Conqueror, at least, had no fear about enlisting them and had evidently contemplated doing so for some time. In a letter to his historian brother, Sir William, dated the 23rd of March, 1844, he wrote[1]*: "I am going to raise two battalions of Scindees and Beloochees as an experiment, without much confidence in them, except against the Sikhs: but a failure will not hurt me, for if they joined an enemy with their arms, two battalions more or less would not turn me out of Scinde."

It was in this spirit that he issued a proclamation for the raising of the first battalion in May, 1844, now "Queen Mary's Own," though he had to wait for two years more before he raised the second. It is worth while to examine the terms of the proclamation to see what was in Napier's mind. The Belooch and Sindee soldiers were to be armed like the sepoys, but instead of the Westernized uniform which was at that time imposed on the unfortunate sepoys of the regular battalions—high shako, stiff-collared coatee, cross-belts, and long white trousers, in close imitation of the highly unsuitable equipment of the British soldiers of the period—the men of this new irregular corps were to be allowed to adhere to their comfortable native dress. The first authorized uniform for the Battalion was the usual Belooch "angrikha" or coat, the "pyjama" or loose trousers of the country and Sindee cap. The last-named is the well-known high hat, of recent years confined to the Amil or Hindu official class, and still worn by members of the Talpur family, but formerly the ordinary headwear of the Sindhi Mussalman. The men were required to serve only within the limits of Sind, and were enlisted for five years. This was in strong contrast to the unlimited service, both as regards locality and duration, for which the soldier of the regular sepoy regiment then engaged. Re-enlistment was, however, always contemplated, and in 1850 Captain Hough, commanding the 2nd Battalion, reported that no mention was then made to recruits of a discharge being claimable after five years

*Figure references are to Appendix II, p. 162.

and that "the men now look on their discharge as a great punishment." The pay of the sepoy was to be seven rupees a month (which was the pay of the regular sepoy at this time), and they were to receive an angrikha and a cap annually. Above all, and most important for the classes to be enlisted, it was formally announced that "every man may wear his hair, beard, and mustachios as he pleases." It was added: "The new regiment must undergo some drill but it shall not be so strict as that the sepoys go through."

These orders seemed admirably suited to overcome local prejudices and attract local men, and steps were immediately taken for the formation of the Regiment at Karachi, though it was announced that enlistments could also be made with the officers in charge of the police at the other large towns of Sind, Hyderabad, Shikarpur and Sukkur. Yet it is clear that difficulties were experienced in obtaining men, or at least the local Beloochees and Sindees who were desired. Nor is this a matter of surprise. As has already been noted, the Ameers of Sind had not maintained any standing army; and there was ample employment in agriculture for the inhabitants of a thinly populated land. Recruitment, moreover, was in the big towns where those seeking employment had come from Afghanistan, the Punjab or even Hindustan; those places, in fact, from which the soldier-adventurers of that period came. Colonel Edward Green, Deputy Adjutant-General of the Bombay Army in 1856, noted in that year that he had known the Belooch battalions from the time they were raised until 1853. He says that as with most new levies it was difficult to keep the men together and that "in the 1st Battalion a large draft of Pathans chiefly men from the Eusoofzaie Country and the Upper Punjab was brought down as a nucleus to the Corps." In spite, however, of initial difficulties, the Regiment must quickly have taken shape, because it was barely twenty months old when it had its first opportunity of going on service. It is interesting to compare this period with the months it took to train extra battalions of the Regiment in both world wars. The aggression of the Sikh Khalsa had made war with the Punjab inevitable; Napier, who had long regarded such a war as certain, and was thirsting for further military glory, was called on to assist the Governor-General, Lord Hardinge, and the Commander-in-Chief, Lord Gough, by marching an army up from Sind. The Government of Bombay sent the necessary reinforcements, and by great personal exertion Napier had a force of from twelve to fifteen thousand men ready in Upper Sind early in January, 1846. In this force the Belooch Battalion was included. Colonel Edward Green, in the memorandum already quoted, says that "the men appeared ready for any work and were confident and contented." It was no small compliment for so young a unit to be included in a force which was recognized to be a very fine one, ready to undertake any task under so inspiring a leader as Sir Charles Napier. The men of the Battalion were, moreover, under no obligation to share in the campaign, since it was to be conducted beyond the limits of Sind, within which only they had undertaken to serve. That they volunteered and were accepted so readily is a proof not only of their morale but of Napier's confidence in them. To the intense disappointment both of Napier and of his men, the Battle of Sobraon was fought and won before the Sind force could enter the Punjab, and Lord Hardinge decided to make peace without annexing the Punjab, or finally destroying the Khalsa Army. Thus the Sind force did not advance farther than Bahawalpur and the Battalion soon afterwards returned to its quarters in Karachi.

It must have been during this training for war that the famous "chikor" incident occurred. For the uninitiated it should be explained that the chikor (more accurately *caccabis chukor*) is a partridge, the most common small game bird found in Baluchistan. In fact, its habitat extends from Cyprus in the west to China in the east, and it is found in all the intervening countries, Arabia, the Persian Gulf, Aden, Mekhran and the North-West Frontier Province of India, the same territories visited so frequently by all Baluch battalions later. It is an extraordinarily mobile bird either on the wing or on foot. Its mixed grey and stone coloured feathers give it perfect camouflage against the barren background it prefers; its call—"chikor, chikor"—is easily adaptable to human speech. They have nests of eight to ten eggs, and later in the season the small covey join packs of from forty to a hundred birds.

It was probably a combination of these soldierly qualities— mobility over any ground, quick concealment, rapid communication, dispersal and concentration at the right place and time— which provoked Sir Charles Napier when inspecting the Battalion during training to observe: "These Baloochies are as quick as their own chikor." The flattering remark stuck and became literally a feather in the caps of their officers, who still proudly wear a chikor hackle on the left side of their service head-dress. It is an unusual badge, a gamekeeper's decoration, to the ignorant more acceptable in mufti than in service dress, and as such the cause of alarm and even despondency among newly arrived general officers wedded to normal dress regulations. I understand that one famous Commandant, as late as 1924, was hauled over the coals by a senior commander for wearing "shikar feathers" in his hat. Unhappily this Commanding Officer did not remember Napier's famous dictum, but, righteous in his cause for regimental tradition, declared flatly that the right to wear the chikor hackle had been granted by Her Majesty Queen Mary. This silenced the senior officer effectively, but has given rise to another tradition not in strict accord with the facts.

It is necessary to record the names of the officers who achieved the task of getting the Regiment into shape with such promptitude. In those days the regular Indian infantry battalion had nominally a full complement of some twenty British officers, though often as many as half of them were away on civil employ, in departmental jobs, or with irregular corps. The Belooch Battalion was, however, only a local corps and as such had only three officers, a commandant, a second-in-command, and an adjutant-quartermaster. Those selected by Sir Charles Napier were Major John Jackson, of the 25th Infantry, Captain Wright, and Lieutenant George Mayor, of the 25th Native Infantry also. Major Jackson had commanded his regiment at Meeanee after its commandant, Major Teasdale, had fallen, and at Hyderabad, and had taken part in the forced march to Umarkot. The 25th was called by Napier "my favourite Sepoy regiment," and it still bears his name. Jackson was specially selected by Sir Charles to raise the Belooch Battalion. He remained with it until 1849, after which year he left it to command his old regiment, the 25th. Captain Wright left the Battalion in 1846 to raise the second battalion, and Lieutenant Mayor remained with it until his death on the 31st of August, 1851: he had commanded it since the departure of Major Jackson.

The ranks and conditions of service of officers of the Indian Army in the pre-Mutiny period deserve more than passing notice. Promotion, judged by modern standards, was grievously slow. Colonels had service ranging from forty to fifty-three years; lieutenant-colonels thirty-five to thirty-nine years; majors thirty-one to thirty-five; and captains eighteen to thirty years. Retirements were effected by the juniors purchasing out their seniors. For instance, a junior major of the Bombay Artillery would receive anything up to four thousand pounds as an inducement to retire. This buying-out money was subscribed by all officers junior to him, and was generally procured on loan from an Indian banker. As the historian Montgomery Martin puts it: "This [practice] is said to be one of the causes of the pecuniary embarrassments which prevail among the juniors of the Indian Army; the buying-out of old officers is, however, deemed essential to efficiency; and it is proposed to legalise the procedure by act of parliament."

We may assume, therefore, that these original officers of our Battalion, despite their apparently junior rank, were experienced veterans of many years' service.

The formation of the second battalion (now 4th Battalion The Baluch Regiment) in June, 1846, fulfilled Napier's original intention of raising two battalions. This occasion has a special interest for our Battalion, not merely as showing that the experiment of the 1st Battalion had proved successful but as the beginning of that famous corps with which our Battalion has always been so intimately connected. It would appear that the difficulty of local recruitment had decreased in the two years which had passed after the raising of the 1st Battalion, since Colonel Edward Green observes that "it will be found, I think, on enquiry that there are many more Pathans and Brohooes in the 1st than in the 2nd battalion."

In January, 1847, the Regiment had its first move from Karachi to Hyderabad, thus beginning the system of interchange between stations in Sind which was to last, except when the Regiment was on field service, until 1893.

The minute[2] of Sir George Clerk, Governor of Bombay, who saw both the battalions in 1848, may again be referred to as showing their condition and constitution in that year. He states that each battalion numbered about eight hundred men and cost annually about one and a quarter lakhs of rupees. The intention of rendering the British service attractive to the military classes of Sind could, however, be fulfilled only if the Corps were composed of men of the province and no others. The returns of the two battalions showed that only about two-fifths of the men of the battalions were inhabitants of Sind, and only one-tenth of the whole could be classed as Beloochees. While, therefore, satisfied with the appearance of the battalions in their lines and on parade, he desired that the attention of the commanding officers should be directed to the original object in raising them. The same point was emphasized in a letter[3] from the Adjutant-General, Bombay Army, in 1851 in which he observed that, in addition to Afghans and others from the Punjab and Peshawar, there were from seventy to a hundred Hindostanees in each battalion. This may, perhaps, afford some justification for a marginal note by John Jacob in a copy of Sir William Napier's account of his brother's administration. "The Belooch battalions were then composed almost wholly of Patans and Hindostanees." The returns called for in 1856 show that in the 1st Battalion nearly five hundred of the eight hundred men came from Sind and Baluchistan, and in the 2nd Battalion about the same figure from Sind alone. As Jacob pointed out in criticizing these returns, it did not follow that men belonging to Sind were all Sindhis or Baluchis. It seems probable, however, that, as local connections increased, local recruitment improved and the outside element decreased, though it always remained strong in both battalions.

Meanwhile, however, the battalions steadily progressed in efficiency, as we may judge from the inspection reports, from which some quotations may be made. Thus Brigadier De Rinzy, commanding in Upper Sind, writes rather ungrammatically on the 21st of March, 1850: "On the 19th and 20th inst, I took the annual inspection of the 1st Belooch Battalion. It affords me great satisfaction to state that I never knew so favourable a result arise from so unpromising a beginning. I witnessed for a long time the formation of these battalions and confess I thought it a hopeless case. My surprise may therefore be judged when on minutely inspecting this one, I found it fully equal in point of discipline and good order to the generality of regiments of the Line, with the advantage on its part of being composed of men in general physically superior being for the most part Patans from the hill parts of Affghanistan, stout, able-bodied men, fit for any work, and admirably adapted for Light Infantry if on trial they prove good men and true. They are well, uniformly, and suitably clothed and armed. The manœuvres in the field were executed with precision steadiness and celerity fully equal to any other regiment, as well as the firing and target practice." It may be observed here that throughout its history many inspecting general officers came to damn and left to praise.

Similarly, in 1851 Brigadier-General Manson reported: "I saw this Regiment for the first time and it, like the 2nd. Regiment, is composed of a fine body of men well dressed, well set-up and from the peculiarity of the dress forming an imposing spectacle. The average height of the Regiment is something over five feet, seven inches. . . . It is fit for the performance of any duty that may be required from it."

It is pleasing to note in view of John Jacob's later strictures, that the General could add as follows: "The almost entire absence of crime from this Regiment for a long period speaks well for the attachment of these men to order and discipline, while the great decrease in desertion evinces confidence in the Government."

The inspecting officer in 1853 stated that he had much cause to be pleased with the 1st Belooch Regiment, "which marches with the firm steady pace of the British soldier." In 1856 Major-General Scott reported: "Collectively to the best of my judgment there are few regular Battalions which could surpass this regiment in the accuracy of its movements. Finally I consider this establishment to have attained a high state of efficiency and to be fit for any service that can be required of it consistently with its organization as an Irregular Corps."

The reports on the 2nd Battalion are equally complimentary, though it may perhaps sound curious to the modern soldier to read that musketry was thought satisfactory when "At the ball practice parade 6 men from each Company at the distance of 100 yards put in 1 hit to 2 misses."

It is especially pleasing to note that the number of offences was not unusually large, and the men are stated to be "cheerful and obedient," and "amenable to discipline, and good tempered."

General Manson describes the "peculiarity of the dress" which formed an imposing spectacle in 1851 as follows: "They wear a red Kilmarnock bonnet, dark-green tunic with a red collar and cuffs, the rest of the coat being quite plain, and scarlet pantaloons." It will be remembered that when Sir Charles Napier issued his proclamation raising the Regiment in 1844 he permitted the recruits to wear the garments peculiar to the province. This must have been always extremely unmilitary in appearance;

and the Sindhi cap must in particular have been singularly unsuitable for the Pathans, Hill Baluchis or Brahuis, and Hindustanis, who, as we have seen, formed a large proportion of the Battalion at the beginning. We may assume, therefore, that a more soldierly dress was quickly adopted. It may, perhaps, be accepted also that the attractive combination of green and red in the uniform was adopted because of the popularity of these colours in Sind, and indeed in other Mohammedan provinces. This combination still, for example, forms the State colour in Khairpur, the surviving Talpur state. It may perhaps surprise those accustomed to the pugri as the universal wear of Indian line regiments to read of Kilmarnock bonnets being worn. (This bonnet was the name generally given to the round forage "pork-pie" cap worn by other ranks in the British Army, and in the Indian Army before the Mutiny. It was smaller than the true Kilmarnock bonnet, which is that now worn by the Royal Scots.) But these were the days when helmets and shakos were worn by the regular Indian regiments of cavalry and infantry in full dress, and soft, round caps in undress uniform.

The spirit that animated both battalions is shown by their volunteering, in spite of the limitation of service in their enlistment, for the distant overseas campaign in Burma in 1852.

We may briefly note some of the changes among the officers that occurred in this period. Lieutenant Mayor died on the 31st of August, 1851, and was succeeded temporarily by Captain Heyman, 15th Regiment, Native Infantry, until Captain Holmes joined. In 1853 the latter was succeeded by Major R. Farquhar, of the 6th Regiment, Native Infantry. Ensign John Watson was appointed Adjutant in 1851, but he was a born cavalryman and left it in the following year for the Punjab Cavalry, with which he was to win the Victoria Cross and great distinction in the Indian Mutiny. He was succeeded as Adjutant in June, 1852, by Lieutenant H. Beville, who thus began his long and distinguished connection with the Regiment.

CHAPTER TWO

1856—1866

A FEW years later a crisis arose threatening the disbandment of both young Belooch battalions. Such crises have been met time and again by all units of the Indian Army, caused generally by the opinions or prejudices held, too often fanatically, by senior officers regarding the martial capacity of the various enlisted classes. Very few officers who serve their lifetime with Indian troops can avoid forming personal likes and prejudices for the various types of races enlisted, and in most mixed regiments one will find a healthy rivalry between the classes for honour in peace and war. This friendly competition, however, merges into a perfectly integrated unit when the honour or safety of the battalion is affected by any outside, hostile, element.

Unfortunately in this interesting episode we have no record of Lieutenant-Colonel Farquhar's reactions to the disbandment proposal made by such a formidable antagonist as the Acting Commissioner of Sind. That his arguments were vigorous and sustained in the best Baluch tradition we may assume; that they were powerful and persuasive enough to be successful we are thankful. The story is a curious one.

In 1856 Lieutenant-Colonel John Jacob, as he then was, who had been for nine years in charge of the Sind frontier, was appointed to act as Commissioner in Sind in the place of the permanent incumbent, Bartle Frere, who had gone on furlough. He lost no time in addressing[1] the Government of Bombay, to suggest that the two Belooch battalions should be disbanded. Mr. Frere had already reported that, so far as their usefulness for internal security was concerned, the work could be done more cheaply by an increase in the number of the police. But John Jacob went farther: he asserted that the battalions were not only unnecessary but a public danger. He wrote: "The men of these battalions make a most imposing display when under arms on parade, but long experience and actual observation of facts convince me that they are disorderly in peace and worthless in war. I feel certain moreover that they are not only worthless, but that on trial they would prove more dangerous to friend than to foe.

"The men are enlisted to serve for five years only. A great portion of the members of the Corps is composed of Brahooes, Affghans, and other tribes residing beyond our territory. After their discharge they return to their homes so that we are in fact forming the men of Beloochistan and Affghanistan into trained soldiers at the rate of three hundred men per annum.

"In case of these so-called Belooch Battalions ever being required for service, they will probably be employed against their brethren on our North-Western Frontier when, it appears to me, that we may in all likelihood find traitors in our camp and a host of our own trained soldiers against us.

"It appears to me in short that we are in fact paying largely in peace for weakness in time of war."

To this drastic proposal the Headquarters authorities of the Bombay Army naturally demurred. They pointed out that Colonel Jacob had no personal experience of these battalions. They observed that the battalions had shown an excellent spirit by volunteering for service whenever possible, and that they had been reported upon in the most complimentary terms by inspecting officers. It was also indicated that both battalions had a large proportion, over sixty per cent., of men who had their homes in Sind, even if these were not all Beloochees or Sindees. It was suggested also that the rate of annual discharge was not nearly so high as Colonel Jacob supposed. The Deputy Adjutant-General, Colonel Edward Green, writing with long experience of Sind and of the battalions, pointed out that they had always performed their duties properly, though he strongly recommended that recruitment should be restricted to Sindees, Beloochees and Pathans residing in Sind. He added: "We have known too many instances of the treachery and blood thirstiness of the Brohees, the Pathans of Affghanistan and the Beloochees beyond the border to wish for their services as soldiers. The latter indeed appear to be of the tribe of Ishmael, their hands against every man, and every man's hand against them."

Colonel Jacob was, it need hardly be said, unconvinced by the views of the authorities at Headquarters. He doubted whether all those shown as belonging to Sind were really connected with the province, and regarded the entertainment of "foreign mercenaries" as dangerous.

It is indeed an irony that one whose name was to be linked subsequently with another Baluch regiment, and so many of whose relations were later to be so honourably connected with the Baluch battalions in general, should have advocated their early abolition. But Jacob, with all his wonderful qualities, was a man of the strongest predilections and prejudices. Among the most bitter of the latter was his dislike of Brahooees (in which term he included all hill Baluchis) and Afghans. Three years before the date of his letters regarding the Belooch Battalion he had recorded these opinions:[2]

"Every Brahooee (the Belooch of Khelat) whom we enlist is certainly either a thief, a coward, or a traitor. The Affghans are more ferocious but have far less real courage than the Hindoostanee: they have more cunning and less intellect: they have more muscular development with far less endurance. But these Affghans etc. are also utterly faithless, and we can never feel a just confidence that they will be true in the hour of need. The Hindoostanee Mussulman has a high feeling of honour—these men have none whatever."

Much more to the same effect can be found in Jacob's writings. He certainly acted up to his principles by forming his Scinde Irregular Horse entirely from men of the Deccan and Hindustan, and ultimately entirely from the latter. It is one of the compensatory ironies of fate that, so soon after his letters were written in 1856, the Hindustani Mussulmans were to show the utmost faithlessness (though the men of Jacob's own Scinde Horse remained loyal), while not merely the Belooch battalions but the purely Baluch Horse enlisted by Macaulay on the Sind Frontier were to display most entire trustworthiness. What Jacob and those who thought like him failed to recognize was the value of another source of recruitment distinct from the races of Hindustan which had begun to think themselves indispensable to the Indian Army. Fortunately the Belooch battalions were shortly to dispel such fears in the most effectual possible manner by their behaviour not only in the Persian War but in the far higher test of the Mutiny.

It was to the 2nd Belooch Battalion that the first chance of field service came in the Persian War of 1856: but the campaign may briefly be noticed both on account of the close connection between the two battalions, and because the battle honours won by the 2nd Battalion in the campaign are now the common property of all the battalions of the Baluch Regiment.

The battle honours were, indeed, somewhat cheaply earned, four being given, though the fighting was in no case severe: in fact, the honour given for the capture of Bushire celebrated an almost bloodless victory. The war itself arose out of the threat made by Persia, doubtless at the instigation of Russia, against Herat, and was declared on the 1st of November, 1856. In the division which first went to the Gulf was the 2nd Belooch Battalion which had, of course, volunteered for this overseas service. This force captured the strong fort of Reshire on the 9th of December with fifty casualties, and Bushire the next day with no casualties at all. The Belooch battalion was engaged on both occasions with a loss of two men killed. Sir James Outram then arrived to command the force with a second division, among whom was John Jacob with eight hundred sabres of his Scinde Horse. The force early in February made a long, forced march to attack the Persian army, which retreated, allowing its camp and stores to be destroyed. Outram's army was followed up and attacked on its return march to the coast, and faced the enemy at Khushab on the 8th of February. Once again the hostile army gave way so rapidly that only the 3rd Bombay Cavalry and the Poona Horse had any opportunity of distinction, of which they richly availed themselves, the total casualties during the night attack and subsequent action being only eighty-three killed and wounded. The Belooch battalion was not engaged in the operations on the west side of the Gulf, being left under Jacob to hold Bushire. A quotation may be given to show how the Belooch soldiers struck an officer of a regular Bombay battalion. "The troops having left for Mohammerah," he writes,[3] "I was placed in command of one of these redoubts, with some gunners and a company of the Belooch Battalion. These men are fine, martial, wild-looking fellows, and might be aptly styled the 'Zouaves' of our Indian Army, for they also, like those gentry, have very elastic notions of *meum* and *tuum*." This comparison is more complimentary than might appear at first sight, because the Zouaves of the French Army were at this date regarded as famous fighters after their exploits in North Africa and the Crimea.

The success of Outram's operations quickly brought the Persian Government to terms, and peace was concluded. A considerable number of troops, however, including the 2nd Belooch Battalion, the Scinde Horse and Jacob himself were left at

Bushire, to ensure that Persia fulfilled the terms to which she had agreed. The greater part of these had not returned to India when the storm of the Mutiny of the Bengal Army broke over the land.

Thus began the warfare in which our Regiment was to win its first, and one of its most distinguished, battle honours. It is not necessary to go into the causes of the Mutiny at length. It will be sufficient to indicate how critical was the position in Sind, how great was the courage with which the Commissioner, Bartle Frere, sent away his most reliable troops, and how important was the response of the 1st Belooch Battalion to his confidence in it. It is well known that the Bengal regiments proved disloyal almost without exception. There was almost the same temptation to the Bombay regular regiments to be equally untrustworthy. They contained three main elements: Brahmans and Rajputs from Upper India, Hindustani Mohammedans, all of these the brethren of the mutinous Bengal sepoys, and the Marathas. Strenuous efforts were made to undermine the loyalty of these classes, and in Upper India it was believed that the Bombay Army would go the way of the Bengal one, although the Bombay officers had profound confidence in their men which proved to be well justified. The Persian War had deprived Bartle Frere of one of his Belooch battalions, of one regiment of Scinde Horse and, above all, of General Jacob, whose name was sufficient to keep the unruly tribes on the Frontier in order. He had in addition a notoriously ill-affected Bengal regiment, the 6th Irregular Cavalry, at Jacobabad, in the place of the Scinde Horse, on service in Persia. That his Bombay men were not free from contamination was proved by the mutiny of one of his four infantry battalions, and both the companies of Native Artillery, though these mutinies took place in different stations, were partial and ill-supported, and were suppressed largely by the other loyal Bombay soldiers. Bartle Frere might well have hesitated before denuding himself of troops on which he could rely. Yet he at once resolved to send his only European regiment, the 1st Bombay Fusiliers, and the 1st Belooch Battalion to assist John Lawrence in the Punjab. There was some delay owing to the ill-prepared condition of the Indus flotilla, but Frere was able to write[4] on 28th May, 1857, to Lord Elphinstone, Governor of Bombay: "The Beloochees were to leave Hyderabad today. Colonel Farquhar says they are highly flattered at being employed." This was the best answer possible to the doubts of Jacob and others regarding their reliability.

The officers who accompanied the Battalion were Colonel Farquhar and Lieutenants Bannerman, H. Hicks and F. W. Knight. Hicks (Pasha) was the officer who later was to attain fame by his gallant death when his Egyptian army was overwhelmed by the Mahdi in the Sudan. Lieutenant Nicholetts, who had been serving with the Scinde Horse in Persia, rejoined on the 9th of July, and Lieutenant H. Beville, who was on furlough in England, in the middle of November.

The Regiment went by steamer to Sukkur, where they halted in case they were required to deal with the Bengal Cavalry Regiment at Jacobabad. When that corps had been secured they proceeded to march towards Delhi through the hottest part of India in the height of summer. They reached Multan on the 8th of July. Here the Left Wing remained under Lieutenant Nicholetts to assist the 1st Fusiliers in looking after two disarmed but still dangerous Bengal regiments. The Right Wing and Headquarters, under Lieutenant-Colonel Farquhar, marched on the 15th of July towards Ferozepore to escort the siege train to Delhi. It is necessary to emphasize the vital importance of their task. The hope of securing British India depended on the early capture of Delhi, where the bulk of the mutinous sepoys had collected and the Mogul Emperor held his puppet court. The doubtful loyalty of the Punjab and many of the Indian States, as well as the wavering fidelity of troops tainted with mutiny, could not be expected to withstand much longer delay. But the little British force on the Ridge at Delhi could not take the walled city held by trained soldiers ten times their number without the siege train that was being collected from the arsenals. Yet the need of men in the Punjab was so great that it was only possible to guard the train on its march to Delhi by this wing of the Regiment, little over three hundred strong, and a few men of Her Majesty's 61st. The train itself was under the command of Lieutenant W. J. Gray, of the Bengal Artillery, with only four European non-commissioned officers. The little force which the historian Holmes refers to as "a weak native detachment" left Ferozepore on the 10th of August and reached Delhi on the 4th of September, two hundred and sixty-eight and a half miles distance, by twenty-three stages in twenty-six days, serious delay having been caused on crossing the Rivers Ghaggar and Markanda, both swollen by monsoon spates. The difficulty of escorting a convoy of six hundred and fifty-five bullock carts, which were constantly breaking down, and was fully six miles long, may be imagined. There was, moreover, the danger of attack by the enemy, who were fully aware of the importance of the train and of its impending arrival. The rebels in Delhi did indeed dispatch a formidable force to intercept it on the 24th of August, but Nicholson, with a portion of the besieging army, followed and overtook this force and destroyed it at Najafgarh. On the 29th of August the train joined a detachment of two hundred and sixty men of Her Majesty's 8th Foot on their way to Delhi, and the combined force safely reached the British camp early on the morning of the 4th of September.[5]

The arrival of the train was naturally received with the greatest enthusiasm by the besieging army. Lang, of the Bengal Engineers, voices the general spirit in his diary: "The Siege Train is here at last. Hurrah for that: now we may begin at last. Now, Mr. Pandy, you may as well shut up." In language singularly like that used by Captain Maude, of the Bombay Army in the Persian War, he expresses his feelings at seeing the men of the Regiment. "The Beloochees, too, have come in, such strange wild-looking fellows: bright, dark green, laced with red, red caps with green turbans. I hope they are plucky and ferocious."[6]

Preparations for using the heavy guns and assaulting the city were immediately begun. It was not long before the Belooch Battalion came into action. On the 7th of September the enemy attempted to prevent the construction of a battery in the Kudsia Bagh. The Beloochees were used in repelling them, and lost Lieutenant Bannerman, shot through the head, the first officer of the Battalion to be killed in action.[7]

The batteries were pushed on with feverish activity and the assault was ordered for the early morning of the 14th of September. There were three assaulting columns, and a fourth operating on the right against the village of Kishenganj. Our Battalion was in the reserve column under Brigadier Longfield, of Her Majesty's 8th Foot, which was to afford assistance whenever required. It consisted of:

	Strength
Her Majesty's 61st	250
4th Punjab Infantry	450
Wing, Belooch Battalion	300
	1,000

in addition to three hundred of the Jhind contingent and two hundred of the 60th Rifles, who, after covering the advance of the assaulting columns, joined the reserve.

Although our Battalion did not take part in the actual assault, it had plenty of occupation on that eventful day. The 4th, or Reid's column, on the right had been unsuccessful and had retired after Reid had been disabled, and the Belooch Battalion was sent to support it.[8] The Cavalry Brigade had suffered severely in remaining exposed to the enemy's fire in order to check a hostile attack. A party, eighty men strong, of the Guides Infantry, working in support of the cavalry, were surrounded by the enemy. They were extricated and brought away by a detachment of the Belooch Battalion under Colonel Farquhar.[9]

Though the three assaulting columns had successfully stormed the walls, they received severe checks in their further advance, and had lost one-third of their numbers. The city was reduced only after six days of steady fighting. In this the Belooch Battalion took its share. On the 16th the important position of the Magazine was stormed by the 61st and our Battalion with but slight loss.

By the evening of the 20th the city was in the hands of the British. The loss suffered by the Battalion in this fighting had been one British officer, one Indian officer and seven men killed, and one missing; and forty-eight men wounded—not a small percentage out of a strength of little over three hundred men.

The fall of Delhi had a tremendous moral effect, and there were also tangible results for the Indian soldiers engaged. It has been said that the people of the Punjab believed in the triumph of the British only when they saw the loot taken by their men in Delhi. Similarly, old Baluch pensioners used to tell civil officers in Sind up to the end of last century tales of the loot that was found: their only regret was that so little of it was in a portable form.

Much work, however, remained to be done. Lucknow and Agra had still to be relieved, Rohilkhand and Oudh had to be reconquered, and communications had to be established with the new Commander-in-Chief, Sir Colin Campbell, advancing from Allahabad, and with the Bombay columns who were seeking to subdue the rebellion in Rajputana and Central India. The capture of Delhi had scattered the mutineers over the surrounding districts, and it was here that the Battalion was first em-

ORIGINAL COLOURS OF 1st BELOOCH
(Now preserved in Windsor Castle)

ployed. The Right Wing, under Colonel Farquhar, moved to the Bulandshahr district, and operated within it for some time. A column under Colonel Seaton joined it most opportunely at Gangari on the 14th of December, as a large rebel force was marching with the intention of crushing Farquhar. The mutineers attacked in ignorance of Seaton's arrival, and were defeated with heavy loss after a severe struggle in which the cavalry of Seaton's force, the Carabiniers and Hodson's Horse, did great execution.[10]

It was now the turn of the Left Wing of the Battalion to see active service. It had, as we have seen, been left at Multan to assist in guarding mutinous Bengal regiments. When relieved of that duty it had been attached to a movable column in the country round Amritsar, and then marched for Delhi in November, 1857. It left Delhi early in January, 1858, to join the column which was being formed at Meerut under General Penny to assist in the pacification of Rohilkhand. Before that task could be undertaken Sir Colin Campbell had to relieve the garrison in the Residency at Lucknow, to rescue Windham and defeat the Gwalior contingent at Cawnpore, and finally to recapture Lucknow itself and to drive the rebels from its vicinity. When this had been accomplished by the 20th of March he could turn his attention to Rohilkhand. Penny's column, in which, as we have said, the Left Wing of the Battalion was included, marched to Fatehgarh, where it met the Commander-in-Chief. Leaving him again and crossing the Ganges for Budaon, the column was attacked at Kakraoli during a night march on the 29th of April, and, though the enemy was scattered, Penny was killed. He was succeeded by Colonel H. R. Jones, of the Carabiniers, and the column again joined Campbell on the 3rd of May, in time for the severe action at Bareilly on the 5th. Here the wing was in the first line in support of the Highland Brigade. The action is chiefly memorable for the fierce onset of the Ghazis, who were destroyed by the 42nd Highlanders, the enemy being scattered with a loss to the British of fifty-eight killed and wounded.

Meanwhile, the Moulvi of Fyzabad, one of the ablest of the rebel leaders, had attacked the small force which Campbell had left at Shahjehanpur, and the Left Wing of the Battalion was in the column which Campbell led by forced marches to its relief, which was effected on the 11th of May. From Shahjehanpur Campbell made a forced march to Fatehgarh, with a small escort of Irregular Cavalry and of the Left Wing of the Battalion—an operation of great danger, as the Moulvi, with a strong force of rebels, was in the neighbourhood. A thirty-hour march was made in extreme heat, the infantry being said "not to have a leg left."[11] This was hardly surprising, as we are told that the Beloochees marched as fast as the cavalry. The Left Wing held the fort of Jelalabad from the 12th of June to the 9th of July, when it marched to Budaon. In these operations the Battalion had no loss of officers, but Lieutenant Edward Willoughby, of the 10th Bombay Infantry, who had been seconded to the Regiment, was killed in the unsuccessful attack on the fort of Ruiya in April.

Rohilkhand had thus been recaptured, but there remained the heavier task of reconquering Oudh, where, in addition to the mutinous sepoys, many of the landholders with thousands of retainers had risen in rebellion.

Sir Colin Campbell, now Lord Clyde, made his preparations for this task with his usual methodical care. The Right Wing had now marched from Bulandshahr and joined the Left Wing on the 7th of September, the Regiment being very strong in numbers. It was attached to the column of Brigadier-General E. Wetherall, C.B. On the 21st of October the fort of Badri was captured, and on the 3rd of November Wetherall, without waiting for General Hope Grant, with whom he had been told to co-operate, attacked the strong fort of Rampur Kessia, the stronghold of the Khanpooria Clan. The fort was taken after an obstinate struggle, the British loss being seventy-eight killed and wounded. Colonel Farquhar and four companies of the Regiment took part in the assault, the Colonel dying shortly afterwards from wounds received in this action.

In addition to him, the Battalion lost nine killed and thirteen wounded. Lieutenant Nicholetts took over command of the Regiment until the return in January, 1859, of Lieutenant H. Beville, who had been in command of the 13th Punjab Infantry. In his despatch Wetherall wrote of Colonel Farquhar: "I was thus deprived of the services of an old, gallant, and experienced officer at a most critical time." On the 18th of November the column joined the Commander-in-Chief and shared in the capture of Shankarpur, which the rebel commander Beni Mahadeo evacuated. He was, however, brought to action at Dhundio Kerria or Bidhua on the 24th of November and completely defeated. The enemy were thus driven over the Ghogra River, and the Regiment marched to Lucknow, escorting the heavy guns.

Now in General Horsford's first brigade, and joining the Commander-in-Chief again on the 5th of December, the Regiment took part in actions at Baraitch (17th December), Nanpara (23rd) and Barjidia (26th). It was in this last action that Lord Clyde, owing to his horse falling, dislocated his shoulder and broke a rib. Russell, the famous *Times* correspondent, relates the following characteristic incident. In the evening the Commander-in-Chief, with his arm in a sling, was sitting on a charpoy in the midst of the Beloochees. "Once as he rose to give some order for the disposition of the troops, a tired Beloochee flung himself full length on the crazy bedstead and was jerked off in a moment by one of his comrades. 'Don't you see, you fool, that you are on the Lord Sahib's charpoy?' Lord Clyde interposed. 'Let him lie there; don't interfere with his rest,' and took his seat on a billet of wood."

The next day, the 27th, the strong fort of Masjidiah was taken. The Left Wing of the Battalion was left to destroy the fort, and the Right Wing returned with the rest of the force to Nanpara. From here, on the night of the 29th of December, the Commander marched through the forest, surprised the enemy at Banki, and drove him across the Rapti River into Nepal territory. Thus Oudh had been cleared of rebels, with much labour but comparatively insignificant loss. The Right Wing returned with the main body to Lucknow, but the Left Wing remained in Horsford's Brigade at Siden ku Ghat to watch the remnants of the enemy in Nepal territory. At the request of the Nepal authorities, the Brigade crossed into Nepal, after scattering the enemy at Sakla Ghat, and held the Soonar Valley for some days.

The Mutiny continued to smoulder through 1859, but the main work was done, and our Battalion could return to Sind. The Right Wing and Headquarters marched with Lord Clyde's force to Lucknow and thence to Delhi by way of Cawnpore, from which place it once more furnished Lord Clyde's escort. Before reaching Delhi it was rejoined by the Left Wing. It had a long journey of one thousand four hundred miles by road and river to cover before its Right and Left Wings reached Hyderabad on the 20th and 30th of May respectively, the Regiment having thus been almost exactly two years absent on service.

Recruitment had been well kept up during the campaign, in spite of the calls for the numerous other regiments that were being raised. The strength of the Regiment was one thousand

and thirteen at Rampur Kessia, and it numbered one thousand and forty-two rank and file on its arrival at Hyderabad, an immediate reduction having to be made to bring it to the peace strength of seven hundred. The number of medals issued to Indian ranks was one thousand one hundred and eighty-four.

How valuable had been its service may be judged from the terms of the General Order issued by Lord Clyde on the 20th of February, 1859:

"1. Her Majesty's 64th Foot and the Belooch Battalions are about to return to the Presidency of Bombay from whence they came to assist in the restoration of order after the outbreak of mutiny and insurrection in that of Bengal.

"2. The Services of both these Corps have been admirable. The Commander-in-Chief is happy in being able to congratulate them on the termination of the last year and half in which they have alike rendered signal service to the State and won great honour for themselves.

"4. The Belooch Battalion took part in the Siege of Delhi, in the Campaign of Rohilcund and in that of Oudh for the reduction of the Province.

"5. Both regiments have been frequently engaged. The Commander-in-Chief wishes them a hearty farewell."

Nor were other recognitions of the good service of the Regiment lacking. In September, 1858, the 1st and 2nd Belooch Regiments were converted from "Local or Provincial" corps to "Extra" regiments of the line. This gave the men all the status and privileges of the Regular soldiers, as well as a pension. On the other hand, it involved the liability to unlimited service instead of the right to claim discharge at the end of five years. Over four hundred of the Regiment elected to take the option of resigning when they had completed this term.

Five Indian officers received the Order of Merit for their services in the Mutiny. Of these, Subadar Seo Charau Misr, whose name shows him to have been an up-country Brahman, served as Native Adjutant throughout and died from the effects of his exertions. The "Shamla," the ornamental flare of the pugri, dates from this period. It is a regimental tradition that the right to wear it was granted because of gallantry and good service during the Mutiny.

The services of other battalions then or afterwards connected with the Regiment may be noted. The 2nd Belooch Battalion had on its return from Persia to be retained for a time in Sind. In November, 1857, it moved to Sukkur on field service and thence to Dera Ghazi Khan, from which place it furnished many guards along the Western Frontier.

A third Belooch battalion was raised at Hyderabad. When the Rajputs at Nagar Parkar, on the east of Sind, rose in rebellion in 1859, this battalion formed part of the force which suppressed the rising. The Mutiny also gave John Jacob the opportunity of putting into effect a project which he had long cherished.[12] This was to raise two battalions on the Silladari principle in force in the Irregular Cavalry. The men were to receive a higher rate of pay, but had to pay for their arms and accoutrements and for a share of the cost of a permanent transport establishment, thus rendering the Frontier Brigade entirely self-sufficient. Two regiments were thus raised in 1858, and were called the 1st and 2nd Belooch Rifles. They were the only Silladari Infantry ever formed in the Indian Army.

The honour of "Central India," now borne by the Baluch Regiment, was earned for it by its present 1st Battalion, then the 24th Regiment, Bombay Infantry, which played a most distinguished part in Sir Hugh Rose's great campaign. The present 2nd Battalion, the then 26th Bombay Infantry, was, after its return from the Persian campaign, employed in quelling small risings within the Bombay Presidency.

The Baluch Regiment as a whole can therefore look back with the utmost pride on its record in the Mutiny.

The inevitable post-war reductions led to the disappearance of all regiments not absolutely necessary. Our Battalion was, in 1861, brought into line as the 27th Native Infantry, or 1st Belooch Regiment, in place of the 27th Infantry, raised in 1846, which had mutinied at Kolhapur. The 2nd Belooch Battalion was similarly numbered as the 29th Native Infantry, or 2nd Belooch Regiment, in place of the 29th, also raised in 1846, which had shown itself very shaky at Belgaum, and also disbanded, though it had afterwards done good service at Aden. The 1st Belooch Rifles were numbered as the 30th Jacob's Rifles, in place of another 30th Native Infantry, which had, in 1858, been formed from the loyal portion of the 21st, the regiment which had partially mutinied at Karachi. The newly formed 3rd Belooch Battalion and the 2nd Belooch Rifles were disbanded.

The establishment of European officers, which had been three when the Corps was on an irregular footing, was increased to six, the number then fixed for all Indian infantry battalions.

As a final mark of the Battalion's services in the Mutiny, the battle honour "Delhi" was bestowed upon it.[13] It is indeed curious that no recognition was made of the long campaigns after the fall of Delhi, but such distinctions were very sparingly granted after the Mutiny. The first record of Colours being presented to the Regiment was in 1862.

It is interesting to note that the sister battalion, the 2nd Belooch Regiment, was sent, in 1862, to China on field service. It is curious, in view of later developments, to find that two companies were furnished for legation duties and protection at Yokohama, Japan. After their tour of service in the Far East, the 2nd Battalion visited the Seychelles Islands and Mauritius, thus considerably extending the area in which the fitness of the Belooch Regiments for foreign service was displayed.

As the 30th Jacob's Rifles were now localized at Jacobabad, the Regiment's stations were confined to Hyderabad and Karachi. Service for eight years in these places was pleasantly disturbed by a warning for field service in Abyssinia received in August, 1867.

CHAPTER THREE

1867—1889

DURING the next twenty years our young Battalion, already forged and tempered in the fierce fires of the Mutiny, became a veteran blade ready in skilful hands as a weapon to fight anywhere where the expanding British and Indian Empires required loyal and resourceful infantry to secure their frontiers. Ten of these years were spent in peace stations in Sind where, there can be no doubt, that magnificent regimental officer Beville kept officers and men hard and fit for whatever task might befall. When one muses back in retrospect to the almost incredible Abyssinian campaign, to the strident alarums and real excursions of the Afghan War of 1878, to the reinforcement company which journeyed to Egypt to add "Tel el Kebir" to our laurels, and to the two years' jungle fighting in Upper Burma, the historian can only mourn that so little in the way of detail, of daily existence, of toil and hardship, of even fun and games, has been recorded for posterity. What a saga of endurance, of bravery and of good humour those hidden years conceal! We can only sketch in the gaunt bones of historical facts, clothing them meagrely with the rags and tatters preserved for us by pious adjutants which hint at, but cannot resurrect, the daring and enduring splendour of those days.

The 1867 campaign against Abyssinia, or rather against its King Theodore, was due to the misdeeds of that monarch, who, in addition to innumerable acts of cruelty upon his own subjects, seized and imprisoned many British subjects and refused to release them. The difficulties of a campaign in such a mountainous and inhospitable country were well known and were, indeed, magnified by popular rumour. The Government of Great Britain decided, however, that an expedition was necessary, and wisely entrusted the conducting of it to Sir Robert Napier, the Commander-in-Chief of the Bombay Army. He deliberately chose Bombay soldiers to form the bulk of his force. He had seen their fighting qualities in the Second Punjab War and the Indian Mutiny, and was well acquainted with them as Commander of the Bombay Army. His advanced brigade, consisting of the 3rd Bombay Cavalry, the 10th Infantry, two companies of Bombay Sappers and Miners, and the Bombay Mountain Battery, landed on the 21st of October, 1867, at Zula in Annesley Bay, some miles south of Massowah on the Red Sea, the spot selected for the disembarkation of the force. They worked arduously in their waterless surroundings until our Regiment and the 3rd Scinde Horse arrived on the 5th of December, to be followed in a few days by the Commander of the Brigade, Sir Charles Stavely.

The men were at once put on fatigue duties and were soon split up into small detachments employed on the difficult task of making roads over the passes for the force, which included elephants and heavy guns. The work of "F" and "G" Companies on a portion known as "The Devil's Staircase," which was made passable only after six weeks' laborious toil, was especially praised by Sir Robert Napier, who had arrived on the 2nd of January, 1868. On the 25th of January Napier was able to begin his advance and reached Adigrat, nearly a hundred miles from Zula. Here the Left Wing of the Regiment was employed in entrenching the post while the Right Wing advanced to Antalo, about half-way to Magdala, Theodore's capital, one hundred and sixty-five miles distant. On the 12th of February Napier continued his advance with the Right Wing of the Battalion, three hundred and twenty-seven strong, in the 1st Brigade. A height of eleven thousand feet had now been reached, and the troops, marching "light scale," with no kit beyond what the men could carry, experienced extreme heat by day and frost by night. Finally, the force struggled up to the Talanta Plateau within striking distance of the peak of Magdala. On the 10th of April, at Arogi, Theodore's fighting men descended to attack the British brigade, of which our Right Wing formed part. The Abyssinians fought with great courage, but were easily repelled with between two and three thousand casualties. The British loss was only twenty wounded, two of them mortally.

The Left Wing, two hundred and eighty-six strong, which had been left at Adigrat, made a forced march under great difficulties which the official record describes as "a march unparalleled in the campaign." It was a few hours too late for the action at Arogi but was in time for the final assault on Magdala. This was not long delayed, taking place on the 13th of April. Magdala was then a hill fort on an isolated rock standing three thousand three hundred feet above the surrounding plain. The gateway of the fortress was taken without great difficulty and, Theodore shooting himself, the conflict ceased, the British loss being only fifteen wounded. The strength of the Battalion in the assault was five hundred and fifty-four.

Napier, having achieved his object and liberated the captives, began his return journey on the 19th of April. It proved to be almost as trying as the advance, since the Abyssinian tribes hung upon the flanks and rear, and the transport animals died off rapidly. The Regiment was with the rearguard throughout, under the immediate eyes of the Commander-in-Chief. Zula, the port of embarkation, was not reached until the 2nd of June. Before the Regiment sailed, Sir Robert Napier visited the two ships in which it had embarked, and thanked the men for their services, speaking in Hindustani. One passage in his speech much have appealed particularly to the sepoys. The General said: "When we arrived at Magdala I was very sorry that your Left Wing was not with us. I missed them very much. When on the night before the storming of the fortress my attendant told me that the Left Wing had marched into camp I said, 'Now all is well; my Beloochees are here.' "

The good work of the Regiment did not fail to receive recognition. The Commandant, Major H. Beville, was promoted to lieutenant-colonel and made a C.B. The Second-in-Command, Major G. F. Hogg, was also promoted lieutenant-colonel. The Subadar-Major, Samueljee Israel (his name shows him to have belonged to the Bene-Israel of the Bombay coast), was admitted to the Order of British India. Finally, the Regiment, along with the 3rd and 10th Bombay Infantry, was ordered to be clothed, equipped and designated as Light Infantry.

Among the spoils of war brought back to India was a silver ceremonial Christian cross which, it is believed, Napier presented to the officers of the Regiment after the fall of Magdala. The origin of the cross—now the most treasured possession in the officers' mess—and its three companions, one other silver cross and two brass replicas, is obscure. One of the brass replicas is known to be in the possession of the 4th Hodson's Horse, but the whereabouts of the remaining two have not been ascertained.

The cross is a beautiful example of Early Christian design and workmanship made of beaten silver with primitive line drawings on each side depicting the Madonna and Child and the twelve apostles. Inside the supporting column are the remains of the wooden shaft on which it was, presumably, carried at high festivals. This magnificent trophy is now mounted on a silver plinth and exhibited only on great occasions.

Thus ended a campaign which Fortescue, the historian of the British Army, declares to be perhaps the most difficult and dangerous enterprise in which that Army was ever engaged. He gives his reasons for this opinion and adds: "The problem was solved, partly by the strong will of the Commander, partly by the extraordinarily fine spirit shown by the troops, both British and Native. Never were men more hardly worked nor subjected to greater privation and hardship, and it must be remembered that all exertion was the more exhausting to them owing to the rarefaction of the air on the upland. Yet, though heavily loaded and traversing terrible ground, they never failed and never complained, accepting cold, wet and hunger with equal cheerfulness. Their discipline was as fine as their spirit, and both were wholly admirable." When one visualizes that great march from the Red Sea to the heart of Abyssinia and the appalling conditions of the return journey, the battle honour "Abyssinia" holds a new significance.

There followed ten years, from 1868 to 1878, of the greatest quiet which the Regiment ever enjoyed. It was stationed at Karachi and Hyderabad in rotation. This period of calm was terminated by the outbreak of the Second Afghan War. That war was primarily due to the intrigues and promises of the Russian Government, which sought to embroil Afghanistan with the Indian Government in view of the probability of war between Great Britain and Russia on account of the terms of peace which the latter sought to impose on a defeated Turkey. Owing to the refusal of the Amir, Sher Ali, to receive a British envoy at his capital after he had entertained a Russian mission, war was declared on the 20th of November, 1878. In its earlier phases the Bombay Army had little share in this war, as the Indian portion of the forces in the field were drawn from the Bengal and Punjab Frontier Armies. Even the South Afghanistan Field Force which, under Sir Donald Stewart, advanced from Quetta to Kandahar, consisted mainly of troops from the Bengal Army. It included, however, the 29th Infantry (2nd Belooch Regiment), while the

EARLY CHRISTIAN CROSS
BROUGHT FROM MAGDALA, 1867

30th Jacob's Rifles were among the troops stationed between Quetta and Kandahar. The first successful phase of the war was concluded by the Treaty of Gandamak. The murder of the British Resident, Sir Louis Cavagnari, and his escort at Kabul renewed hostilities. Kabul was successfully occupied by General Roberts. In the south, Sir Donald Stewart reoccupied Kandahar, and sent a brigade to reconnoitre the Kabul road as far as Kalat-i-Ghilzai, where the 2nd Beloochees were left in garrison. The fighting round Kabul was so severe that it was decided that Sir Donald Stewart should march with his division to strengthen the force at Kabul, being replaced at Kandahar by a division of the Bombay Army.

The Regiment had moved to Jacobabad in October, 1878, and furnished detachments at Sibi, then a frontier town, and other places on the lines of communication. When it was decided to hold Kandahar with Bombay troops the Regiment was ordered to proceed on service in Southern Afghanistan in March, 1880. Unfortunately the division sent to Kandahar was weak in numbers, and the higher command was singularly inefficient. Further, General Primrose, the divisional commander, was directed by 'the new-fangled telegraph" in Simla from the Political Department of the Government of India to detach a brigade, including the 30th Jacob's Rifles, to support the troops of the Wali of Kandahar, whom the Indian Government had set up as a ruler independent of Kabul, and to watch the very much larger force of disciplined troops which Ayub Khan, the brother of the deposed Amir Yakub Khan, commanded at Herat. The separate employment of this brigade was made in spite of General Primrose's protest emphasizing the inadequacy of his numbers, and against the opinion of Army Headquarters. The Wali's troops quickly mutinied and deserted, but General Burrows, who commanded the detached brigade, was ordered to intercept Ayub Khan at all costs, the Government of India being solely anxious to prevent Ayub Khan from marching on Kabul, and being apparently oblivious of the danger to Burrows's brigade and to Kandahar itself. As a result, Burrows felt himself obliged to attack Ayub Khan when he reached Maiwand on the 27th of July, 1880. The disparity of numbers was very great, Burrows having just over two thousand five hundred men, including his sick, while Ayub had eight thousand regular troops and three thousand irregular cavalry, with thirty-two guns manned by trained artillerymen, and of much heavier calibre than Burrows's guns. In addition, Ayub Khan had at least fifteen thousand tribesmen and Ghazis, who proved themselves most formidable opponents in the battle. There can be no doubt that the higher leading of Burrows's brigade in the action was inept and marked by great indecision, the handling of the cavalry force being particularly feeble. The men as a whole fought well, but the task demanded of them was too great. Outnumbered, outgunned and outflanked, disaster overcame the small British force. The losses of those engaged were nearly thirty-three per cent. in killed alone, a large proportion of the casualties being incurred in the disorganized retreat. The small garrison of Kandahar was quickly invested, but prompt action was taken to retrieve the disaster. From the army at Kabul a picked force of ten thousand men was detached under Sir Frederick Roberts, while Phayre was directed to collect his scattered regiments and move on to Kandahar. It is unnecessary to describe Roberts's well-known march. At Kalet-i-Ghilzai he picked up the 2nd Belooch Regiment, and this corps shared in his brilliant victory of the 1st of September.

The efforts made by General Phayre and the corps under him, in which our Regiment was included, to reach Kandahar are worthy of record. He was hampered by want of transport, the great heat, the absence of grain and fodder owing to a two-year drought, and the necessity for carrying supplies for the Kandahar garrison and Roberts's force. The tribesmen also made many petty attacks. Roberts's arrival at Kandahar and his defeat of Ayub rendered it unnecessary for Phayre to hasten the last stages of their march. The many difficulties on the way had been overcome by the excellent spirit displayed by the force.

After the return to India by way of Quetta of Sir Frederick Roberts's force and of the original Kandahar garrison, that latter city and district continued to be held by a force commanded first by General Phayre and later by General Hume. Our Regiment belonged to this force, and had to do much marching through the district, including an expedition to the melancholy field of Maiwand.

Peace had been concluded with the Amir Abdurrahman, who succeeded in overthrowing all his rivals, but the evacuation of Kandahar did not take place until April, 1881. Our Regiment left it on the 20th of April, and reached its destination, Hyderabad, on the 18th of May.

For its services the Regiment was given the distinction "Afghanistan, 1879-80."

Two events of Regimental interest had occurred in these years. In January, 1881, Colonel H. Beville, C.B., retired, after a connection with the Regiment of twenty-eight years, for twenty-two years and three months of which he had commanded it. Truly he could say in his farewell order that the Beloochees had a reputation second to none in India. His name is still commemorated by the generous bequest he made of a considerable sum of money to be used for the widows and orphans of Indian ranks, known as the Beville Fund.

In April, 1879, Subadar-Major Samueljee Israel had retired, after forty years of service, thirty-five of which had been with the Regiment since its formation.

In 1881 the 30th Jacob's Rifles was reconstituted and designated the 3rd Belooch Regiment, thus forming a direct connection with the older Belooch Regiments which has ever since been maintained. A quick result of this connection was that Jacobabad became a station for all three regiments, probably even in those hard days a doubtful privilege.

In 1882 chronic misgovernment in Egypt led to a military rising under Arabi Pasha. It was necessary to send an expedition, including a contingent from India. The 2nd Belooch Regiment formed part of it, and was joined by "G" Company of our Regiment under Captain J. Grant. The 2nd Regiment thus earned the honours "Egypt, 1882," and "Tel el Kebir" which are now borne by the Baluch Regiment.

In the year 1886 signs of the reorganization of the Indian Army began. Regiments being linked together in threes, our Regiment was naturally joined with the 2nd and 3rd Belooch Regiments, the 29th and 30th of the Bombay Line. Enlistment for five years (subsequently reduced to three) with option of extension was substituted for unlimited service, and a beginning was made in the formation of regimental reserves.

A word may be said about the recruitment of the Regiment in this period. We have seen that the original intention was to obtain men who were resident in Sind, and, when the two Belooch battalions became line regiments in 1858, it was repeated that recruits should be obtained from the neighbourhood of their permanent headquarters. In 1873 the restriction to recruitment in Sind was relaxed, and enlistment, under the "general mixture" system was thrown open to all classes possessing the necessary physical requirements. This brought into the Belooch Regiments a larger element of Sikhs, Punjabi Mohammedans and Pathans. In 1885 it was ordered that enlistment should be restricted to inhabitants of Baluchistan, Pathans of the Zhob, and transfrontier Pathans from countries and tribes to the west of Jacobabad. This involved cessation of recruitment in the Punjab and the transfrontier areas bordering on that province. In practice we are informed that this prohibition was generally ignored.

The next call to our Regiment for active service came in October, 1886. In the previous year the misgovernment of Theebaw, King of Burma, his numerous outrages against British subjects, and his intrigues with the French made the dispatch to him of an ultimatum inevitable. This he treated with contempt. On the 14th of November, 1885, the British force crossed the frontier. The resistance was nominal, the war was ended in a fortnight, and on the 1st of January, 1886, the country was annexed to the Indian Empire. This, however, only began the real trouble. The robber bands which had long been a feature of the country were reinforced by the disbanded soldiery. The guerrilla resistance of these bands lasted for nearly five years and was so formidable that at one time about thirty thousand regular troops were employed against them. Our Regiment was among those called to this scene of warfare. It left Hyderabad on the 3rd of October, 1886, under the command of Lieutenant-Colonel G. C. Sartorius (strength eight European officers, fifteen Indian officers and seven hundred and sixty rank and file), reached Rangoon on the 14th of October and at once proceeded to Upper Burma. Then followed a warfare the general pattern of which has not changed even in modern times, a warfare of detachments and small posts in which the junior commanders, both European and Indian, had ample opportunities for distinguishing themselves, which they fully grasped. Especially good work was done by the Mounted Infantry, of which two companies, afterwards reduced to one, were formed from the Regiment. With the Mounted Infantry, Lieutenant (afterwards General Sir Michael) Tighe and Jemadar Ram Sing (killed in action) deserve especial mention. In 1888 the Regiment was moved into the Shan States, where they again split into detachments, covering a large area of country. In December of that year the Regiment, five British officers, seven Indian officers and three hundred rank and file, besides the

Mounted Infantry company, marched as part of the Karen Expeditionary Force into the Red Karen country. It was with this force that on the 1st of January, 1889, Surgeon J. Crimmin, the Medical Officer of the Regiment, won the Victoria Cross, the first officer of the Bombay Medical Service to receive this award. This was the Regiment's last expedition in the campaign. It left Burma on the 15th of April, 1889, and reached Karachi on the 29th of April after two and a half years of arduous campaigning. Its services may be judged by its losses, by the distinctions it earned and by the praise given to it. It had lost one British officer, three Indian officers and eighty-four other ranks killed or died of wounds or disease, while five British officers, four Indian officers and a hundred and fifty-one other ranks had been invalided to England or to India. The distinctions bestowed, in addition to Surgeon Crimmin's Victoria Cross, were the C.B. and brevet colonelcy to Lieutenant-Colonel G. C. Sartorius, the Distinguished Service Order to Captain A. L. Sinclair and Lieutenants M. J. Tighe and F. J. Fowler, and five Orders of Merit to Indian ranks. Among the numerous tributes of praise from general officers may be selected that of Major-General (afterwards Field-Marshal) Sir George White, who commanded in Burma. "I have formed a very high opinion of the soldier-like qualities of this Battalion. The native officers and men are active, fond of enterprise, and capital campaigners." It was an additional gratification to the Regiment that Lieutenant-General H.R.H. The Duke of Connaught, at that time Commander-in-Chief of the Bombay Army, should, in January, 1890, have thanked all ranks on parade for the manner in which they had, by their services in Burma, upheld the good name of the Bombay Army. The campaign honour "Burma, 1885-87," was granted to the Regiment in 1891.

Three small changes may be noted as having occurred in this period. The Karen expedition was the first on which the Regiment wore khaki clothing. The official designation was changed from 27th Regiment, Bombay Light Infantry (or 1st Belooch Regiment) to 27th Regiment (1st Belooch Battalion), Light Infantry: a small alteration but one ending the old separate numbering of the Belooch Regiments. On the return of our Regiment from Burma in 1889 the 29th (2nd Belooch Battalion) was moved to Loralai, the first occasion on which a Belooch Regiment served outside Sind, except when employed on field service.

CHAPTER FOUR

1889—1908

THE next eight years until October, 1897, was a time of comparative quiet for the Regiment. It took its turn of duty at Karachi and Hyderabad and in 1893 succeeded the 2nd Belooch Battalion at Loralai, its first station in time of peace outside of Sind. It supplied detachments at Jacobabad (which did not cease to be an Infantry station until 1898) and in many parts of Mekran, which was being brought more definitely within the orbit of the Indian Government. For ten months of 1894-95 it supplied the greater part of the escort for the Boundary Commission which was settling and demarcating the boundary between Baluchistan and Afghanistan, the historical Durand Line, the entire work of erecting the boundary pillars being done by the escort. Although one of the objects of the original formation of the Regiment had been the maintenance of order in Sind, it was not until 1896, more than fifty years after its formation, that it was called on to assist the civil power in the province. A serious outbreak by fanatics called Hurs, the followers of one of the Sind Pirs, proved to be beyond the capacity of the civil police to control. Three parties of the Regiment were employed to aid the well-known Deputy Commissioner of the district, Mr. W. H. Lucas. These parties had several brushes with the outlaws, and experienced some losses, but the trouble was effectively put down until 1942, when the 6th Battalion of the Regiment was similarly engaged.

Throughout these years the Regiment continued to receive excellent reports from the officers under whom it served: as, for example, when Sir George Luck, Commanding the Quetta District, described it as "a regiment which he has always considered to be the *'beau ideal'* of efficiency, smartness and soldier-like bearing."

Though the Regiment was not actively engaged in this period, the 2nd and 3rd Belooch Regiments were part of the Zhob Field

Force which subdued the Sheranis in the rugged neighbourhood of the Takht-i-Suleman.

Although these years were externally peaceful, there were many signs of coming internal changes in the Army. One of these was the conversion in 1891 of the 24th and 26th Bombay Infantry Regiments into battalions localized in Baluchistan, and recruited from the tribesmen, mostly Pathans, living within or on the borders of the Baluchistan agency. Both the old Bombay regiments had a long record of loyalty and good service. The 24th, for example, in addition to the campaign honour "Central India" to which we have already referred, carried "Aden" on its colours for its share in the capture of that fortress. With the spread of law and order in India, however, and the disappearance of all internal elements of disturbance, the centre of military gravity had shifted to the North-West Frontier, and it was natural that regiments recruited from the fine fighting material there available should to some extent replace the down-country regiments. These two Baluchistan regiments were destined to become the 1st and 2nd Battalions of the Baluch Regiment. At the outset, however, they had no connection with the three existing Belooch battalions, though it may be noted that after the change the 24th received as their first commanding officer the very well-known Commandant of Jacob's Rifles, Colonel M. H. Nicholson. He took with him as adjutant of the reconstituted corps an officer who had already served with him for six years as Adjutant of the 3rd Belooch Battalion and was afterwards to be famous as Field-Marshal Sir Claud Jacob. Nor were changes lacking in the organization of our own Battalion. In 1892 the "class company" system, already in force in some of the regiments of the Bengal Army, was introduced in place of the "general mixture" organization, and recruiting was extended to the Derajat and Trans-Indus territories. Under this sanction, companies came into being consisting of Afridis (Adam Khel), Khattaks (Bangash), Yusufzais (Transfrontier) and Mohmands (Cis Frontier). In 1896, orders were received that the three Baluch Regiments should be constituted of four companies of North-West Frontier Pathans, two companies of Hill Baluchis (including Brahuis and Derajat Baluchis), and two companies of Punjabi Mohammedans. The Regiment by this constitution was classified as follows: "A" and "B" Companies, Baluchis and Brahuis; "C" Company, Orakzais; "D" Company, Afridi Adam Khels; "E" and "F" Companies, Punjabi Mohammedans; "G" Company, Yusufzais Transfrontier; and "H" Company, Mohmands, Cis Frontier. The establishment was eight rifle companies, each a hundred strong. It will be observed that the last cursory connection with Sind by local recruitment disappeared under this organization.

In 1893 came a greater change in the abolition of the old Presidency armies which came into effect from the 1st of April, 1895. The reform was long overdue, as the independence of the local armies had ceased to be more than nominal while it had prolonged the existence of many administrative drawbacks. In the Baluch Regiments, at least, this break with old tradition could have caused little regret, as their distance from the seat of Government in Bombay and Poona had rendered their connection little more than perfunctory. The abandonment of the old and comfortable rotation of stations in Sind and the consequent severance of old ties must indeed have caused regret: but the increased contact with other armies and the wider experience of larger stations must have been conducive to efficiency.

Another lesser change may be noted. The military authorities at last gave way to the pressure of more accurate orthography and the time-honoured spelling of "Belooch" gave way to "Baluch." By the same order the abbreviated title for ordinary use, "the 27th Baluchis," was officially approved.

In the year 1897 the unrest among the Afridi tribes and the consequent closing of the Khyber Pass compelled a reluctant Government of India to take strong action, nearly forty thousand men being put into the field. Our Regiment was ordered to join the 11th Reserve Brigade of the expeditionary force. It reached Rawalpindi on the 10th of October, but a more urgent call soon came to it. On the 22nd of November orders were received for the Regiment to go to British East Africa.

The cause for this summons may briefly be given. The territory known as Uganda had long been rent by internal wars which had compelled the Chartered Company of British East Africa to take forcible measures in 1894 against Kabbarega, King of Unyoro. In 1895 the Charter of the Company was recalled, and the British Government became responsible for the administration. Fighting continued chiefly with Arab princes of the Nazruni family. There was already an Indian contingent in the country, but Nubian or Sudanese soldiers were also enlisted. In 1897 these Sudanese, who had certainly been underpaid and overworked, mutinied, killing three of the British officers. The mutineers were joined by the ex-chiefs of Uganda, Mwanga and Kabbarega, and by the Mohammedan Waganda. This condition of affairs necessitated the summons of our Regiment.

The first Indian unit to serve in East Africa had been the 24th Baluchistan Regiment, now the 1st Battalion of our Regiment, which had gone there in 1896. The disturbances with which it had to deal were, however, in the coastal area near Mombasa.

Our Regiment left Karachi on the 3rd of December, 1897, and reached Mombasa on the 12th. It was under the command of Lieutenant-Colonel W. A. Broome, with Major C. H. V. Price as Second-in-Command. Several of its officers were to rise to distinction, as, for example, Captains M. J. Tighe, F. J. Fowler and W. M. Southey. From the 2nd Baluch Battalion were attached Captain C. O. O. Tanner and Lieutenant J. A. Hannyngton. Of its officers, Captain Tighe had already served with the 24th Baluchistan Regiment in East Africa.

After a brief halt the Regiment, leaving "F" Company to hold Mombasa, went by rail to Indi, railhead of the Uganda railway, at that time in course of rapid construction. Thence it marched by detachments to Kampala on Lake Victoria Nyanza, five hundred and sixty-one miles distant. This place was reached by Captain W. M. Southey with "A" and "B" Companies on the 30th of March.

As each detachment arrived at Kampala it was pushed on into the Unyoro district to relieve the hard-pressed troops of the East African Protectorate. There followed, as in Burma ten years previously, a war of detachments which were employed in hunting down and, when found, attacking the mutineers and the tribes of the Waganda people that had rebelled. The work was extremely arduous owing to the dense jungle and wide-spreading swamps, and the extremes of climate. Food supplies were scanty and uncertain, and for considerable periods the scattered detachments had to live on bananas and sweet potatoes. Nor were the enemy forces to be despised; they consisted largely of Sudanese, good fighters and well armed. It is possible to mention only the principal of the many incidents that occurred.

A detachment under Captain W. M. Southey drawn from "A" and "B" Companies with a section of "D" Company took part in the operations against the mutineers on the east bank of the Nile. On the 26th of April the Sudanese stockade at Mruli was taken after a stiff fight in which the loss among the British regular troops was one British officer wounded and thirty-seven other ranks killed and wounded. Of these casualties the Baluchis' share was one Indian officer (Jemadar Sher Din) died of wounds and five men killed; Subadar-Major Yar Mahmeed and nine others being wounded. The South Unyoro area was cleared by the detachment under Captain Fowler, while North Unyoro was dealt with by Major Price's force.

The mutineers reassembled and stockaded themselves at Jeruba on the western bank of the Nile. A concentration of all available troops was made to attack them, the Baluch force consisting of Major Price, four other British officers, four Indian officers and two hundred and thirty-three rank and file. The attack was successfully carried out on the 4th of August. Lugard describes one of Major Price's exploits in these terms: "Scaling a steep mountain in the dead of night, he surprised a picquet, jumping into the midst of them as they sat round their fire, and overpowering them with the aid of one or two intrepid followers."

Early in October Lieutenant Hannyngton arrived at Kisalize to reinforce the small force of Swahilis at that place. On the 9th he proceeded with two Indian officers and sixty other ranks to place a garrison at Kimanina. On the 10th he was attacked near Kitaba in thick jungle by an overwhelming force of mutineers and rebellious natives, who had crossed from the other bank of the Nile. Hannyngton was severely wounded and his little force was compelled to retire to Kisalize. Jemadar Muhammad Shah and thirteen men were killed. A survivor reported: *"The Jemadar exhorted his men to stand fast and die where they stood, setting the example and fighting to the last, and the men did the same."* Great credit was won by Naik Yusaf Khan, who covered the retirement with a rearguard of seventeen men. In spite of ten of them being wounded, the party retired in good order for twenty-one miles until they reached Kisalize. During the night they occupied a deserted stockade and beat off an attack. For their conduct the whole party received the Order of Merit.

The men awarded the Indian Order of Merit were 2657 Naik Yusuf Khan, 1765 Naik Sultan Mahomed (of the 30th Bombay Infantry, attached) and Privates 2737 Nur Mahomed, 262 Sharif Khan, 20 Ghulam Mahomed, 1441 Nur Dad, 2858 Barkatullah, 153 Shak Zad Shak, 767 Subey Khan, 959 Subey Khan, 188

Khuda Bux Khan, 403 Fazal Khan, 1361 Shazada Khan, 162 Karam Dad, 1132 Mir Tiroz Ali Shak, 295 Sher Dad and 31 Nur Mahomed, whilst it was announced that 296 Private Alimed Khan would also have been decorated had he survived. This wholesale award for a single action is rare in military achievement.

The enemy followed the retirement right up to Kisalize, and made an unsuccessful attack upon the post.

During the concentration that followed, Captain Tighe, with Lieutenant C. V. Price and "G" Company (Yusufzais), marched a hundred and fifty miles in five days, an astonishing performance under the conditions.

A force was quickly collected to deal with the mutineers and rebels. One column under Captain Fowler, including three other British officers, three Indian officers and a hundred and seventy-one other ranks, surprised the enemy, estimated at three hundred Sudanese and five hundred Waganda, and drove them out of their stockade at Kidweri on the Kapa River and across the Nile on the 27th of October. In co-operation with another column under Colonel Coles, of the Uganda Rifles, which included Captain Tighe, two other British officers and eighty-one other ranks of the Regiment, the enemy were again attacked and dispersed on the 25th of November in the Kinjanguti district beyond the Maanja River. On the 21st of December the two columns again met at Kinakulia, the enemy having been dispersed with great loss and driven over the Kapu River into North Unyoro. In the meantime, Major Price, operating from Massindi with Lieutenant Dyke and sixty-five men of the Regiment and one and a half companies of the Uganda Rifles, had dispersed the rebels in the Budonga Forest of the North Unyoro district and had moved down towards the Kupa River. By the 1st of January, 1899, the operations in North Unyoro were completed. Captain Fowler, with his detachment of the Regiment, proceeded to strengthen the posts on the Nile. Early in February the detachments at these posts were relieved by the 1st Uganda Rifles (Indian contingent) and the Regiment concentrated at Kampala. Thence it proceeded by detachments to the railhead, now at Kapiti Plain, which it reached on the 14th of April, finally reaching Mombasa by rail on the 20th.

Meanwhile, "F" and "H" Companies, three Indian officers and one hundred and fifty-four men, under Captain C. O. O.

Tanner, had sailed for Kismayu, to take part in the operations against the Ogaden Somali in Jubaland. Here they spent nearly ten months of arduous service against these troublesome opponents.

The bulk of the Regiment left Mombasa on the 11th of May and reached Karachi on the 20th. The casualties of the Regiment in this arduous campaign had been very considerable, though the losses by disease were not so great as might have been expected. Two Indian officers and nineteen men had been killed in action, and one British officer, two Indian officers and twenty men had been wounded. One Indian officer and twelve men had died of disease, and one Indian officer and fifteen men were invalided. No fewer than ten of the British officers were invalided, or went on sick leave, at the end of the campaign.

The Regiment received the very highest commendation from the authorities, civil and military, in East Africa. It had penetrated farther into the heart of Africa than any other Indian regiment had ever done.

For their services in this campaign Major C. H. V. Price was awarded the Distinguished Service Order, and Captains Tighe and Fowler brevets as major. The Order of Merit was given to eighteen of the rank and file. The campaign distinction "British East Africa, 1897-99," was granted by General Order No. 65 of the 25th of January, 1901.

The medal awarded for this campaign, the East and Central Africa Medal, 1897-1899, is of interest in that it had four bars inscribed "Uganda," 1897-1898," "Lubwa's," "1898," and "Uganda, 1899." Owing to the widespread nature of the campaign the distribution of these medals and bars was uneven throughout the Battalion and the medals themselves were variously inscribed "1st Baluch L.I.," "27 Baluch L.I.," and "27/Bom. Infy." Probably fewer than five hundred of the Battalion were awarded the bar "Uganda, 1897-1898"; for their campaign against the Ogaden Somalis, Captain Tanner's two companies received the "1898" bar; the rare "Lubwa's" bar was awarded to two hundred and forty-three other ranks who happened to arrive in the prescribed areas within the qualifying dates but did not actually take part in the engagement of Lubwa's Hill.

Both the 26th Baluchistan Infantry and the 3rd Baluchis (Jacob's Rifles) took part in the China Expedition of 1900. Two

British officers, three Indian officers and ninety-six other ranks of the Regiment joined the latter, not returning until 1902. These regiments earned the campaign distinction of "China, 1900," for the future Baluch Regiment. The next field service of the Regiment was very near their home country. There was much trouble in 1901 in Mekran, near the Persian boundary, and several of the Baluch sardars of that area went into outlawry. On the 30th of November a detachment of the Regiment under Major Tighe, consisting of two hundred and fifty rifles and three other British and five Indian officers, went by steamer from Karachi to Gwadar, whence they marched to Turbat, where they were joined by a detachment of the Regiment of one Indian officer and fifty rifles who had already been sent there on escort duty. On the 16th of December Major Tighe was requested by the Agent to the Governor-General to attack and capture the strong fort of Nodiz which had been occupied by three leading outlaws and a band of about ninety well-armed desperadoes. Finding the fort too strong to storm out of hand, Major Tighe awaited the arrival of a section of two guns of the Murree Mountain Battery. It arrived on the 20th of December after a forced march, and Major Tighe immediately attacked. After the guns had made a practicable breach, Lieutenant G. P. Grant of the 126th Baluchistan Light Infantry, with Lieutenant Corry of the Bombay Sappers and Miners, led the storming party against it. Both British officers fell severely wounded, and the storming party was checked by a rush of swordsmen. Major Tighe then brought the guns up to point-blank range. After they had shelled the defences effectively, a further assault with the bayonet caused the enemy to surrender. Three men of the Regiment had been killed, and six, in addition to Lieutenant Grant, wounded. After this gallant little action the detachment split into small parties and did much marching with occasional fighting against outlaws and raiders, in co-operation with a Persian force, and at times within Persian territory. Before the detachments returned to Quetta in May, 1902, they had covered on foot distances varying from one thousand four hundred to two thousand miles. For their services in this campaign Major Tighe was promoted to brevet lieutenant-colonel and Lieutenants Grant and Corry were given the Distinguished Service Order, while two Indian officers and a lance-havildar received the Indian Order of Merit.

After this the Regiment was not to have any experience of

fighting before the First World War. It was employed in more than one year in Mekran in attempts to prevent the passage of gun-running caravans from the Persian Gulf to Afghanistan and the North-West Frontier of India. In April, 1906, Lieutenant J. C. Tate, with fifty rifles, made a particularly fine march of sixty-two miles in twenty-two hours in great heat in an attempt to intercept an Afghan caravan. Shortly afterwards Jemadar Raj Wali, with thirty rifles, succeeded in capturing nearly the whole of another caravan. In 1908 the Regiment went by rail to Nushki to co-operate with the 126th Baluchistan Light Infantry in the checking of the arms traffic. An attempt to seize a large caravan failed only because of its escape into Persian territory; but the traffic was prevented from taking the route through British territory and had to follow the longer route through Seistan.

This period of service was most trying owing to the sand-storms and heat and the absence of drinkable water. Such water as was found was full of salts. In one area there was no water at all for forty-two miles; in another nothing drinkable for sixty-five. The Regiment did not return to Quetta until August, 1908.

CHAPTER FIVE

1908—1914

THOUGH there was little campaigning during these years there were many changes in the Indian Army. The arrival of Lord Kitchener in 1902 was the harbinger of much reorganization. The steps already in contemplation for the greater uniformity of the Indian Army and for the reshaping of its commands and divisions were put into effect. Among the changes were the renumbering of the regiments, a reform always exasperating to officers but ignored by the men who for some more generations were to refer to themselves simply as "First Beloochies." Fortunately the old Bombay regiments were lightly dealt with by the addition of a unit to the old number, so that our Regiment in 1903 became the 127th instead of the 27th. Another result of Lord Kitchener's quickening spirit was the Kitchener Test, a contest for efficiency in 1904-05 among all units. The cup was won by our sister battalion, the 130th, the winning marks being 1,395; we were well up the list with a total of 1,367. The 130th owed much of their success in the final tests to the labours of their Commandant, Major F. J. Fowler, D.S.O., who had seen so much service with our Regiment. He succeeded Colonel E. G. Even and became our Commandant on the 28th of January, 1907, a famous tenure of office to which we shall refer later.

There were considerable changes also in this period in the internal constitution of the Battalion. When the double-company system was adopted in 1900 the companies were classified as follows:

No. 1 Double Company.—"A," Afridis (Adam Khel); "B," Orakzais.

No. 2 Double Company.—"C," Yusufzai (Chagherzai); "D," Mohmands (Cis Frontier).

No. 3 Double Company.—"E" and "F" (Hill Baluchis, including Brahuis and Baluchis of the Derajat).

No. 4 Double Company.—"G" and "H," Punjabi Musulman.

In 1910 the Government of India considered the possibility of enlisting large numbers of Mahsuds in the Regular Army with the twofold object of utilizing fine fighting material and of giving lucrative and civilizing employment to the turbulent youth of Waziristan. In the Adjutant-General's Letter No. 1378/6 of the 20th of January, 1911, it was ordered that the Mahsuds thus enlisted should be incorporated in the three Baluch battalions, which would then consist of three companies of North-West Frontier Pathans, three companies of Mahsuds and two companies of Punjabi Musulmans. The recruitment of Baluchis, Brahuis and Yusufzais was to cease for these battalions. Such Baluchis as volunteered were to be transferred to the 124th Baluchistan Regiment on its return from China; in the meantime, the Baluchis in the two linked battalions were to be absorbed in our Regiment. The men of the Yusufzai company were to be transferred to the 130th and to any other corps willing to accept them. The loss of the Chagherzais was keenly felt by the whole Regiment, as they were a particularly fine company, and it is good to record how loyally and efficiently the Yusufzai officers and non-commissioned officers who remained set about training the Mahsud usurpers.

It was not until May, 1912, that the recruitment of Mahsuds for our Battalion began. In that month Major Tanner went to Sarwakai, in South Waziristan, and returned with the son of a malik recommended for a direct commission and sixty-six Mahsud recruits. Tanner, who had experience of the Mahsud temperament in the 129th, wisely selected youngsters all under the age of eighteen and these youths took to soldiering like ducks to water. They astonished the more sedate regiments in Poona by their extraordinary vitality, ready at the end of the most gruelling manœuvres to throw off their equipment and hurl themselves into a vigorous performance of a tribal dance without showing any sign of fatigue. Later the Khattaks were to display a similar virtuosity. The young jemadar Mir Badshah reached the rank of acting subadar-major in the First World War and that of captain in the Second. The slight, bespectacled figure of Mir Badshah (he lost an eye while serving in France in 1915 with the 129th) has been familiar to all Baluch battalions stationed in Waziristan between the two wars. A fine personality with the rugged independent point of view bred in his own clear-cut hills, and the simple directness of the true Pathan, he has always remained the faithful child of "Aik sau sathais" (127).

The gradual elimination of the Baluch and Brahui Double Company was a grievous experience for all who had served with them. Men of splendid physique, inured from birth to a life in which only the fittest survived, often showing a primitive, uninhibited attitude towards both property and sex, they always responded nobly to good leadership, especially when their basic qualities of toughness and loyalty were required. It has already been indicated that, although the original intention had been to form the Regiment from these tribes, they had never provided the majority of its men; the inherent dislike of the nomad for the ordered existence and discipline of a sepoy's life made their recruitment difficult. But they provided many fine soldiers. The last of these was Subadar-Major Yar Muhammad, a Brahui from Kelat, who retired in 1913 after over thirty-five years' service, during half of which he had been Subadar-Major. The rank of honorary captain was conferred on him on his retirement.

If there was little fighting during these early years of the century it was nevertheless a time of distinction for the Regiment. It was chosen for the great Delhi Durbar of 1902-03 as the representative regiment of the Bombay Army. In March, 1906, the Regiment was visited and inspected at Chaman by Their Royal Highnesses The Prince and Princess of Wales, later to become King George V and Queen Mary. New Colours were presented by His Royal Highness in place of those carried by the Regiment since 1878. Her Royal Highness was graciously pleased to accept the old Colours. These were taken to England by the Commanding Officer, Colonel Even, on his retirement in December, 1906, and are now preserved at Windsor Castle. In April of that year His Majesty King Edward VII had sanctioned the addition of the title "Princess of Wales's Own" to the name of the Regiment. When King George succeeded to the throne this title was changed to "Queen Mary's Own," a unique honour in the Indian Army.

In his inspection report for 1905-06 General Sir Archibald Hunter wrote: "This is one of my best battalions. I place great reliance on its fighting qualities. Personally I should always feel safe on service with a body of such officers and men as the 127th Baluch Light Infantry." General Sir Horace Smith-Dorrien wrote in similar high terms.

In December, 1909, shortly after its arrival in Poona, the Regiment received an order to proceed immediately to Somaliland to assist in the evacuation of the administration from the interior to the coast. The fighting anticipated with the Mad Mullah did not materialize, the most serious loss being the disappearance of the regimental baggage in a spate, the gains being the medal and clasp "Somaliland, 1908-1910," and a considerable quantity of rum acquired by a plausible Quartermaster from a credulous Commissariat.

The Regiment returned to Poona in the monsoon of 1910, its first experience of a down-country station. It is a fitting place to pause; to take stock of our condition and to recapture if possible the spirit of Army life in those days, now almost fabulous. Our modern humorists have selected Poona as the comic Valhalla of all retired field officers, its euphonious name making it simple enough for even a B.B.C. comedian to pronounce with some orthoepical distinction. Before the First World War, however, Poona was one of the most important training areas in India and, on account of its incomparable diversity of country and climate, remains so today. In those days the Finance Department of the Government of India had their customary hold on military expenditure, a grasp which rarely relaxes until too late, but a grip it must be admitted equally felt by all parts and components of the British Empire in the ever-fleeting interludes of peace. This perennial financial grip has been experienced by all Commanders-in-Chief from Sir Robert Clive to Sir Robert Cassels, and its reactions are common to all generations of the Baluch Regiment.

This niggardly attitude and its effects may be judged when our "frontier" regiment took over its "John Company" barracks in Poona. These lines were ancient mud-huts built on the *joriedar* system, the men living in pairs in compartments with a common courtyard and door—not dissimilar to the married quarters of an Indian unit from 1920 to 1940. The Government granted a hutting fund for the upkeep and maintenance of the friable fabric of these buildings, and we need hardly stress the loss of training time spent in *"lipaing"* and restoring these dwellings, for which the unit in occupation was held in strict account. The 127th Baluchis, unfortunately, came from a frontier station whose commander had appropriated the hutting fund for his own station's upkeep. When confronted with a demand for payment for the prehistoric huts in Poona, our Regiment was therefore not only unwilling but unable to pay.

The upshot of this temporary bankruptcy was fundamental.

The authorities decided to build new barracks; but, running true to economical form, insisted that the old lines should be demolished, the debris removed to an adjacent fever-breeding hollow, and the whole area levelled by the incoming unit, us. This major work was thoroughly enjoyed by the men, particularly the running of a trolley railway which gave great scope for spectacular collisions and derailments, but interfered continuously with training.

The rationing system then prevailing in the Indian Army also had its roots in the pre-Mutiny era, and merits a brief description. Included in the men's pay was a ration allowance which they were compelled to spend with the Regimental *bunia* and butcher. Cooks, water carriers and sweepers were provided by the State. A company cook collected the *atta* and fuel from the group of men (nominally a section but generally a *handiwal* of village comrades) for whom he cooked and received free chupatties as his perquisite. The *handiwal* cooked their own meat and vegetables when occasion or hunger demanded extra sustenance. There was no real system in the modern sense except this time-honoured custom, supervised benevolently and on the whole efficiently by the company Indian officers. In training and on manœuvres the arrangement was shored up by good man management combined with the uncanny foresight of the Regimental *bunias,* who defied all laws of war and umpires by their camouflaged methods of infiltration and dissimulation. On large-scale manœuvres the meat ration was supplied "on the hoof," and at the conclusion of the exercise it was quite frequently a matter of vain speculation among other units how the Baluch herd had managed to increase its numbers. Like all good shepherds, the 127th probably tended their flocks by night.

Clothing and uniform were also a matter for private enterprise rather than nationalization in India. The accountancy was regulated by a fund called "The Half Mounting," a mysterious name derived it may be from John Company days, when the sepoy provided his own transport also, a Moghul relic perhaps of the Persian system whereby every two foot soldiers provided one donkey for their joint transportation. The system, whatever its origin, made each battalion responsible for the supply, tailoring and upkeep of the men's uniform and mufti. The men received a clothing allowance which was spent under regimental arrangements to buy the cloth, buttons, badges and leather, the uniforms and footwear being made up and fitted by the regimental tailors and shoemakers. In those days a sepoy had one full-dress uniform, two or three khaki uniforms and two sets of regimental mufti. (All afternoon parades and all parades on Thursdays and Sundays were carried out in mufti.) The quality and cut of uniforms under private enterprise were excellent and when, during this period, these were brought under nationalization by Government ordnance factories, the sartorial change was viewed with some dismay by all ranks.

For normal parades officers wore a khaki drill tunic with white shirt, stiff collar and black tie, Bedford cord breeches and gaiters, double cross-belt and sword. This order of dress was, of course, common throughout the Army, which, conservative to a degree concerning dress, was then feeling its way tentatively towards the adoption of shorts for field training. Shorts were a workmanlike enough garment for peace soldiering, but their adoption was opposed by our wholly Mohammedan battalion on both religious and æsthetic grounds. Even a quarter of a century later on King's birthday parades in June, with the thermometer around a hundred and twenty degrees in the shade, when the rest of the Battalion paraded in shirts, shorts and sweat, the Colour party, Indian officers and men, considered shorts unbecoming to their high ceremonial office. With such a splendid sense of dignity and honour no one dare quarrel.

With these upheavals in environment, training and administration the Commanding Officer, now Lieutenant-Colonel F. J. Fowler, D.S.O., was probably impatient, but from all reports this legendary Commanding Officer refused to permit any vagaries of climate, surroundings or higher authorities to suppress his passion for training for war. Fowler was outstanding, among many great Commanding Officers, in his personality for imprinting his ideas and ideals of soldiering on the 127th Baluchis, ideals which were to last long after his command and many ideas which anticipated our most modern military thought. Fowler, like all dynamic leaders, had the idiosyncrasies of character which give rise to stories to be magnified or distorted by the passage of years. The writer therefore hopes that a few tenuous anecdotes will help to illustrate the powerful influence he exercised during his tenure without in any way detracting from the important part he played in our history. During his period of command he twice refused promotion because he loved his regiment.

At this time the tactical training of the Army was uncertain, being an unhappy combination of Egyptian, Boer and Russo-Japanese second-hand information, and depending largely on the predilections of the immediate divisional commander. For instance, tactical drill formations to form square (to repel cavalry), to advance and to retire in echelon were an essential battle drill. Fowler characteristically utilized these compulsory but obsolete movements as close-order-drill parades for which they were admirably suited. For the tremendous biannual ceremonial parades to celebrate the New Year and the King's birthday he had only one rehearsal. At this parade he "damned the battalion into heaps upon heaps of shame-faced officers and men" (one of his subalterns is quoted), and then abjured the assembled battalion in passionate terms: *"Pultan ke waste aur bhi Khuda ke waste achcha karo!"* (For the sake of the Regiment as well as for God's sake, do your best!) At the appointed hour he then led his battalion past the saluting base with the companies in perfect line and rhythm. Such empirical methods would, of course, have failed without the Battalion's background of close-order drill.

His officers and men feared him on parade and respected him in their personal relationships. "Don't be the first company to meet the Colonel sahib in the morning" was a Regimental slogan. One unfortunate newcomer was informed by his subadar one early morning that the look-out men had signalled the arrival of the Commanding Officer from the east, and the subadar suggested marching the squads towards the west end of the parade ground. The suggestion was spurned by the young officer, righteous in his zeal and well-doing. Fowler, bearing down upon him, shrivelled his unctuous soul and his company's uneasy spirit with a wealth of adverse criticism and a torrent of meticulous comment which blasted the young subaltern's every hope of survival. Later, the tempest past, the Indian officers cheerfully explained the obvious prudence of a quick withdrawal when the sentries, posted for the purpose, gave the warning signal. Fowler, it is alleged, had to have one vigorous attack each morning, and the company with which he made first contact was invariably the victim.

At a brigade rehearsal for a ceremonial parade he was impatiently awaiting his turn to lead the Battalion past. Other regiments were being made to repeat their movements, causing considerable delay and some confusion. His ear for music was imperfect: indeed, it is stated that he recognized "God Save the King" only when his neighbours stood up and saluted. For this reason in the disjointed medley of music being performed by the massed bands he had to keep asking his Adjutant "Is that us?" when the bands blared out a fresh tune. After many disappointments the Adjutant said: "That's our march, sir." Fowler, surprisingly, ordered the Battalion to order arms and stand at ease. He then galloped across the parade ground to an astonished bandmaster, and told him in no uncertain terms that his conducting, harmony, tempo and general musical efficiency were beneath contempt and that if he did not smarten up his performance he would refuse to march his battalion past at all. In fairness it should be made clear that Fowler was probably right in demanding a light-infantry pace of a hundred and twenty-four beats to the minute, but his delighted Baluchis only observed the edge being vicariously worn off his early morning temper.

His consuming interest remained in field exercises, and the Battalion, trained to march at four miles an hour over any country, doubling when necessary to increase this pace for some specific tactical object, achieved a great reputation. At this time Poona was the Indian centre for what is now called amphibious and commando training, being also the headquarters of the expeditionary force earmarked for overseas on the outbreak of war. In one of the more spectacular seaborne attacks on the island of Bombay two subalterns, Davies and Quayle, anticipated the Second World War. Davies, disguised as a Parsee, smuggled himself on shore and as a fifth columnist signalled safe approaches to the landing craft. Quayle, demolishing the railway bridge at Andheri, captured the officers' mess of the Bombay Light Horse and made the opposing general (Gorringe) a prisoner. This latter *coup* was ruled out of order by an outraged umpire. The Poona Divisional Commander was a far-sighted leader and approved of these bold tactics. On one occasion he put out of action all officers, regimental sergeant-majors and subadar-majors, leaving the regiments to carry on the exercise under their company Indian officers and non-commissioned officers. The 127th was the only unit to emerge from this severe test with credit.

To those who experienced combat and assault courses in the Second World War, when realism was introduced by the use of live bullets, grenades and ammonal explosions, it may be surprising to know that brigade field firing was a common practice in those "antiquated" Poona days. It must have been a triumph of organization, fire discipline and fire control to see a massed brigade advance to the attack under its own close-support artillery fire thickened with its own machine-gun and rifle bullets. This attack culminated in a terrifying bayonet charge with ranks ten deep. The 127th were proud of their musketry skill. In E. A. W. Lake and other officers they had keen marksmen and instructors who helped the Battalion to "swipe the board" in the command team events, although other units—generally the 80th Carnatics—always managed to win the individual championships.

In those days the officers' mess was literally the officers' home, and in the same way that a battalion's quarter-guard exemplifies to the discerning eye a unit's efficiency and *esprit de corps* the mess was the standard by which the discerning eye could judge the quality of its officers. Since the First World War there has been a gradual relaxation of the complete discipline which encompassed an officer's life in, say, 1912; it is a matter for the sociologist or an army headquarters to applaud, or to deplore, as the case may be. The present historian merely observes the tendency. Certainly the mess in Poona was a proud habitation and guest nights were splendid occasions. It may be recorded that the officers were a temperate crowd given to healthy abstemiousness, a condition made necessary not so much by pecuniary considerations as by the high standard of fitness required for their regimental activities, and supervised closely by the Commanding Officer, Fowler, and his Second-in-Command, Tanner. Strict etiquette was observed in all matters—down to officers being detailed by the mess president to return calling cards personally. This punctilio continued, of course, to a larger or less degree in the between-war years, but its observance became slacker as the "manners maketh man" creed became an exploded theory under democracy's more robust attitude towards social niceties.

The Adjutant was the regimental paymaster and handed the balance of monthly pay to officers after all regimental deductions had been made. At this period these deductions in the 127th Baluchis included a subscription of forty rupees for polo. Many infantry regiments maintained a polo team in those days when this magnificent game was within the scope of anybody able to afford two 14.2 ponies of average ability. Later, when the height of the pony became unlimited to include the faster and heavier importations from England and Australia and, more especially, when the offside rule was abolished, the game became more and more the recreation of cavalry regiments until finally they monopolized it. Under the direction of McCudden, who commanded a cavalry regiment with distinction afterwards, the 127th polo team was in its way famous and, it need hardly be stressed, its excellence was due entirely to hard work and stern training. Each officer personally schooled and exercised his pony for an hour before morning parade and again in the evenings, or practised stickwork on a dummy in the pit. Three afternoons a week the whole station assembled on the polo ground, where up to thirty chukkers were programmed. In the 127th the ponies were supplied by the polo fund and allotted to individual officers for exercising and games. For tournaments they were all at the disposal of the team. To use them on parade required the polo secretary's reluctant permission. Among the stalwarts of the polo team in its heyday were McCudden, Auret, O'Neill, W. L. Maxwell, Tate, Harvey-Kelly, Belli-Bivar and Lake. It was a hard school, possibly unfair in its regard to the rights of individuals who were blessed with neither a good eye for a ball nor a good seat on a horse, but without doubt excellent for health, horsemastership—which an infantry officer neglected at his peril—and for goodfellowship throughout the Service. It may have been due to this tradition of sound animal management that in three separate campaigns in Burma—1888, 1931 and 1943—the Baluch Regiment was commissioned to raise Mounted Infantry, our own Battalion undertaking this role on the first two occasions.

Other events which took place during this period may briefly be recorded. Sind *batta,* an allowance of a hundred rupees a month given to all officers, civil and military, serving permanently in Baluchistan, was abolished. Some years before the option of receiving this allowance, or three months' leave in lieu, had been offered by the Government to the officers of the two Baluchistan Regiments and the three Baluch Regiments; the men had their choice of free rations or a "dearness" allowance. The Baluchistan Regiments chose the hundred rupees and the free rations, whilst the Baluch Regiments favoured the extra leave and the extra allowance. When orders were issued there was some natural chagrin when it was published that the Baluchistan Regiments had been granted both concessions. In 1909 Lord Kitchener issued orders that when the 124th and 126th Baluchistan Regiments moved out of Baluchistan the allowance would cease, and in 1911 sent them both to China.

In November, 1911, the Regiment went to Bombay for the ceremonies in connection with the visit of King George V and Queen Mary, and remained under canvas until Their Majesties' return to Bombay and departure from India in January, 1912.

It will be recalled that it was in this year that the enlistment of Mahsuds began. The Battalion was consequently reorganized so that military training might be more quickly imparted and the regimental spirit instilled into this new element, who were ignorant of regimental customs and traditions and, incidentally, of any language but their own Pushtoo dialect.

No. 1 Company.—"A" Company, Mahsuds; "B" Company, Orakzais (Mulla Khel).

No. 2 Company.—"C" Company, Mahsuds (Manzai); "D" Company, Mohmands (Usman Khel).

No. 3 Company.—"E" Company, Mahsuds (Manzai); "F" Company, Punjabi Musulmans.

No. 4 Company.—"G" Company, Afridis (Adam Khel); "H" Company, Punjabi Musulmans.

Before leaving Poona it would be impolite not to mention the minor riot which the Battalion precipitated in the bazaar. It started when an elderly sepoy of some twenty years' service had an argument with a butcher. The sepoy was a venerable and inoffensive Punjabi Musulman and hardly deserved to be hit with a hatchet. That started the row, which spread as sowars and sepoys of other regiments joined in, with the result that the butchers' bazaar suffered some damage before the men were rounded up and brought back to barracks. Our Battalion received most of the blame; as a punishment they were sent out to camp and then to Somaliland as already recorded. Their good name and reputation were not seriously affected, but the memory of that unfortunate brawl was remembered by the local inhabitants for a generation.

In his valedictory order of the day on the final departure of the Regiment the General Officer Commanding the Poona Division (Sir Arthur Barrett) wrote:

"During its long stay in Poona this battalion has earned a high reputation for general efficiency, smartness and good discipline. On its first arrival here there was a considerable prejudice on the part of the inhabitants against the Pathan soldier. But this has been quite overcome owing to the good behaviour of the men, and the tact and good management of the officers."

On the 17th of February, 1914, the Regiment left Poona for Karachi. It was thus in the original place of its formation when the First World War began.

CHAPTER SIX

1914—1918

BEFORE the fortunes of the Regiment in the First World War are recounted it may be well briefly to consider the organization of the Indian Army at its outset. The changes inaugurated by Lord Roberts and completed or extended by Lord Kitchener had altered, greatly for the better, the personnel, constitution and distribution of the Indian regiments. But neither these changes nor the drastic regrouping of commands and divisions had been tested by war. There were, moreover, serious defects in the regimental system itself, such as the small number of British officers, only twelve per battalion, the non-existence, for any practical purpose, of any reserve of officers, and the paucity and unfitness, chiefly due to age, of reservists for the ranks. These defects were fatally noticeable when the regiments on service were exposed to casualties on a scale unprecedented in any Indian warfare. They could be made good, and then only partially, only by denuding of their best officers and men the regiments not at first sent on service. But these regiments were themselves soon in urgent request for service elsewhere: and in any case the mingling of officers strange to the men, and of drafts of men of different caste, creed and origin from those from which a battalion on service had been formed, immediately impaired its efficiency. Nor was the system of the higher administration of the Army satisfactory. The system which had been described by Lord Kitchener as one of dual control and divided responsibility had been changed for one which placed the whole burden of administration on the Commander-in-Chief. In the words of the Mesopotamian Commission Report, this led to a situation "whereby the combination of the duties of Commander-in-Chief in India and Military Member of Council cannot adequately be performed by any one man in time of war, and the existing organization is at once over-centralized at its head and cumbrous in its duality below."

Still more serious in its effect on the preparation of the Army for war on any large scale was the parsimony, to which reference has been made, with which the demands of the Military Department had been treated by the Financial Department of the Government of India. Formerly the fear of a Russian invasion of India had been some check upon undue economy; but this possibility had been regarded as being eliminated for practical purposes by the Anglo-Russian Agreement of 1907. The result of this economy was that the Indian Army was deficient in much necessary equipment. "The Indian Army was thus to be submitted to a test for which it had neither equipment nor experience."

These general considerations had, however, only an indirect effect at the outset on the Regiment. Fate was not unduly kind to it although the officers present suffered acute disappointment. The Regiment had, as we have seen, left the Poona Division only a few months before the war began. Had its departure been delayed it would have shared in the glories of that division, which fought victoriously in Mesopotamia from Fao to Ctesiphon, and perished honourably at Kut-el-Amara. Further, it had been transferred to Karachi, a defended port of the utmost importance from which early departure was impossible. Again one of its linked battalions, the 129th, was in the Lahore Division, which was immediately sent to Europe. The other linked battalion, the 130th, was shortly afterwards warned for service in East Africa. Its departure was indeed delayed by an untoward incident; but it was always intended to, and after some months did, go to its original destination. These two linked battalions, and especially the 129th, owing to its severe losses on the Western Front, inevitably were a drain upon the strength of the Regiment, both in British officers and Indian ranks. To use a phrase evolved in the Second World War, the 127th Baluchis were heavily "milked" by their sister battalions.

On the outbreak of war the Regiment had to furnish numerous guards at Manora, the strong-point that marks the entrance to Karachi harbour, and at other places in the vicinity of Karachi. The duties thus imposed were heavy and continuous. On the 22nd of August the 129th arrived at Karachi, and embarked on the 24th. Major G. G. P. Humphreys, of our Regiment, with four Indian officers and two hundred and thirteen other ranks, was transferred to them on their arrival in Karachi. On the 1st of November Captain R. D. Davies, with three Indian officers and sixty-six other ranks, was sent to Europe as a draft for the 129th; and these were followed by other drafts later.

It is not necessary to follow in any detail the campaign in Flanders and France in which the 129th added such renown to the name of the Baluch Regiments. It has been admirably described by Captain Thatcher in his book "The 4th Battalion 10th Baluch Regiment in the Great War." It is sufficient here to recall that the Regiment closely followed the 57th Rifles as the first unit of the Indian Corps to be engaged, and had the distinction on the 26th of October near Hollebeke of being the first Indian unit to make an attack upon the enemy. In this Captain Hampe Vintcent was killed, the first officer, it is believed, of the Indian Army to fall in the war. The Regiment was the only Indian unit to receive "Ypres, 1914," as a battle honour. Most notable of all, perhaps, the 129th had the great distinction of having in Sepoy Khudadad Khan the first Indian soldier to win the Victoria Cross. The losses of the 129th in such fighting were necessarily very great. Among those who fell was Major Humphreys of our Regiment. He died of wounds on 30th October. His epitaph is best given in the words of the Regimental Order of the 127th: "By his death the Regiment loses its best officer, and all ranks mourn a loyal comrade." Among the men of our Regiment attached to the 129th there had been a hundred and thirty-four casualties by the reports received in India by the 31st of December.

While, therefore, our Regiment had incessant duty connected with its situation as garrison of a defended port, its main function during the early period of the war was to serve as a training and reinforcing unit for regiments on all fronts. It was ordered to recruit on a large scale, but this was a task not free from serious difficulty. The Mahsuds in various battalions soon began to cause anxiety. There was unrest in their own country: and they believed that an expedition against them would have been undertaken but for the war. In the Mahsud Company in the 124th the Subadar failed to rejoin from leave, and this so upset the company that twenty-two of them deserted when the company was ordered to France as a reinforcement to the 129th. The General Officer Commanding at Poona had remarked in 1913 that their introduction into the 129th was turning out a great success. Yet by September, 1914, the commanding officers of the three Baluch Regiments had represented that three companies of Mahsuds in each battalion were too many, and it was ordered that one of them should be replaced by a third company of Punjabi Musulmans. There followed the bayoneting of Major N. R. Anderson, of the 130th Baluchis by a Mahsud sepoy of his regiment during embarkation at Bombay, and the trouble subsequently caused by the Mahsud companies of this regiment in Rangoon. This led to the recruitment of Mahsuds being stopped, and it was indeed being found impossible to get them. A recruiting party of our Regiment got two Mahsud recruits and lost five of the party by desertion. This cessation of recruitment led to restiveness among the Mahsuds of our Battalion, now reduced, owing to drafts sent to the 129th, to one Indian officer and sixty-two men. All this time no men were fighting better in France than the Mahsuds of the 129th. As Colonel Southey, their Commanding Officer, said: "They seem to revel in the fighting." This excellent conduct they maintained in East Africa. Resumption of Mahsud recruiting was allowed in April, 1915.

Desertion among Pathans other than Waziris, such as Afridis and Mohmands, was also not uncommon. The Regimental records describe it as inexplicable, as the Pathans were certainly not lacking in courage. Similar unrest was, however, found in a Punjab regiment sent to Mesopotamia: and it is probable that it was due to the work of Turkish and German emissaries playing upon the religious feelings of the Pathan soldiers and their relatives.

In December resumption of recruiting of Baluchis and Yusufzais was allowed, and recruiting from the Punjab was, of course, continuous. In spite of the numerous drafts sent abroad, the strength of the Regiment on the 30th of April, 1915, was one thousand two hundred and thirty-six. During this period the Regiment received many officers of the Indian Army Reserve. Several of these came from the mercantile community of Karachi with which the connection of the Regiment had always been most cordial.

In May, 1915, the Regiment suffered what was truly described as a very great loss through the death of Major (Temporary Lieutenant-Colonel) W. L. Maxwell, D.S.O., who was killed in Gallipoli while serving with the Royal Naval Division.

In 1916 the Battalion moved to Calcutta for internal security duties. There the training of drafts, now becoming an incessant drain on the skilled man power of the Regiment, continued.

On the 28th of May, 1917, the Regiment left Lahore for South

Waziristan under the command of Temporary Major J. C. Tate (who had rejoined the Regiment from the Political Department), the Commanding Officer, Lieutenant-Colonel C. O. Tanner, being in command of the Seistan Field Force. Temporary Lieutenant-Colonel A. B. Merriman, who had been on staff duty since the beginning of the war until he assumed command in Calcutta, rejoined on the 1st of June, 1917. Lieutenant-Colonel Tanner, after returning to the Regiment, had again command of a brigade. Eventually, when he assumed command of the Regiment, he was unable owing to sickness to accompany it to Africa, where it went under Lieutenant-Colonel Merriman's command.

Although the Regiment had arduous duties in Waziristan, being on the lines of communication in an advanced position, with much picqueting, they had no fighting. In the middle of July orders were received for the Regiment to leave Waziristan and move to Lahore, where their depot now was, with a view to early embarkation for East Africa. The Regiment reached Lahore on the 6th of August and embarked at Bombay on the 17th. It was intended that the Regiment should leave India with its full strength of one thousand one hundred of all ranks. The men, however, had suffered severely from colitis and malaria in Waziristan, and only about six hundred were passed as fit for service in East Africa. A draft of two hundred and fifty men originally intended for the 130th was therefore picked up at Delhi, as the 130th was, as will be noted below, under orders to return from East Africa to India. Lieutenant-Colonel Merriman had with him Major Nicholas as Second-in-Command, and ten other British officers.

The Regiment disembarked at Kilwa Kissiwani, a port in the southern portion of German East Africa, on the 29th of August, 1917.

The campaign in that country may briefly be described so that it may be possible to judge the position when our Regiment arrived. It had not been intended at the outset of the war to do more than defend the British possessions in the east of Africa from attack. The danger of leaving the German territories to remain as a base for commerce destroyers became manifest, and the Home Government called upon the Government of India to provide a force for their conquest. The somewhat miscellaneous force which was all the Government of India could at the time supply was badly handled and suffered a disastrous repulse at Tanga early in November, 1914. This reverse had a most unfortunate effect in encouraging the Germans to resist, in giving their native soldiers, or askaris, confidence, and in creating prejudice against Indian regiments in spite of the gallant behaviour of the 101st Grenadiers at Tanga. Thus the British position in their own territory was precarious throughout 1915. Among the earliest Indian reinforcements were the 130th Baluchis, who were engaged throughout the year, particularly in March, 1915, at Salaita Hill, a point within British territory. Gradually the British force was strengthened, and in December, 1915, the War Office took charge of the campaign. General Smuts was appointed to command, but before his arrival another severe action was fought at Salaita Hill on the 12th of February, 1916, in which the 130th greatly distinguished themselves by the manner in which they assisted the European South African regiments after these had failed in their attack on the enemy's position. Our other linked battalion, the 129th, had arrived from the Western Front in January, 1916. Both these Baluch battalions took part in General Smuts's offensive which definitely asserted British superiority. The German force was, however, admirably commanded by von Lettow Vorbeck, whose inferiority in numbers was counterbalanced by the fact that his Europeans were veterans inured to the climate, while his askaris were natives of the country carefully trained and of fine fighting quality. The German forces fought on interior lines, were able to choose their positions in healthy country and were well fed. The British forces, on the other hand, were of many races and varying quality, and suffered greatly from the climate.

Smuts's policy was to carry out long turning movements in the hope of encircling the enemy forces. The long marches rendered it difficult to maintain the columns; and more than once German forces eluded encirclement by a failure of portions of the British force to make the final push and prevent the escape of the hostile force at any cost. Von Lettow himself paid the 129th a high compliment when he wrote that "regiments like the 129th Baluchis which had fought in Flanders were no doubt very good," but he pointed out that such regiments could not be expected to stand the fatigues of African warfare for a prolonged period and were later filled with young soldiers. The Germans were greatly aided in their defensive warfare by three considerations: the bush, the black cotton soil, impassable for wheeled transport after rain, and the climate.

Nevertheless, after much marching and fighting, the enemy had been driven out of his ports, railways and important centres by the end of 1916. Smuts, however, had failed to prevent the enemy from slipping through his cordon, and the fighting that remained for 1917 was perhaps the bitterest of the campaign, since the British commanders (including General Van Deventer, who succeeded Smuts in command of all troops in East Africa) realized that the only method for real success was to attack the Germans wherever found at the risk of suffering greater casualties than were inflicted. In the early portion of 1917 the British forces were practically immobilized by an unusually heavy rainfall, and by the lack of transport, which had been exhausted by the exertions of the previous year. By the middle of the year preparations for a fresh offensive were ready. War-worn regiments like the 130th Baluchis, who had borne the heat and burden for so long, returned to India, and were replaced by fresh units, amongst them our Regiment. Most of the South African regiments were also withdrawn, but they were replaced by troops better suited to the climate from other parts of Africa, while the King's African Rifles from East Africa itself had now become a formidable force.

After its disembarkation at Kilwa Kissiwani the Regiment moved to Redhill, about two miles from Kilwa Kivange, where it remained for about ten days to collect kit and porters and also to carry out some training in bush warfare with the Nigerian Brigade, already encamped there. In this it was much assisted by Major Gibb of that brigade, though as it turned out the conditions were to be found to differ in some material respects from those in West Africa. A certain amount of loss was experienced during disembarkation, including the serious one of three or four cases of whisky, which were looted. On the other hand, a box inscribed "Prisoners of War, Kut," found its way to our camp. It was found to contain a hundred pounds of gold-leaf tobacco: most welcome treasure trove which was shared with the 55th Coke's Rifles, who had also come from India. Here the Regiment lost its Second-in-Command, Major Nicholas, transferred to the Kapurthala State Infantry.

Orders had been received for concentration at Massindje and the Regiment marched on the 10th of September with a strength of six hundred men. Lieutenant Wace was left at the base camp with two hundred men. It is some evidence of the unhealthiness of the climate that, when this detachment ultimately joined the Regiment at Ruangwa, though it had had no fighting and no special hardships, it numbered only seventy. On the 15th of September the Regiment reached Massindje, where the Headquarters of the East African Field Force then were. Not a man had dropped out or had to be sent back during the few days' march, which was a mild record in its way, as all other units had dropped some men, such was the trying nature of the climate. The Regiment formed part of the second column, the other units being the 129th Baluchis, the 1st King's African Rifles and the 22nd Derajat Mountain Battery. Later the units were constantly changed, but our Regiment was in No. 2 column throughout.

The general plan of the campaign may briefly be explained. Von Lettow, with the bulk of the German forces, was in the south-east of his territory. Tafel, with his second force, was in the interior in the Mahenge area. It was proposed "to make a combined movement southwards from the Kilwa area, and southwestwards from the Lindi area, engaging the enemy wherever met with." It was thus hoped to encircle von Lettow, to prevent his junction with Tafel, and to cut him off from the south, where the Rovuma River was held by Portuguese troops who, it was fondly hoped, would prevent his crossing. In the meantime, the northern British force, with the Belgians from the west, were to press vigorously against the enemy in the Mahenge area.

The forward move began on the 19th of September against the enemy's position between Ndessa and Mihambia. It was not so strongly held as was believed, as von Lettow had taken a portion of his force to face the Lindi force, which he succeeded in holding up. The position was, however, a strong one, and it was decided that while No. 1 column should attack Mihambia No. 2 column, in which was our Regiment, should turn the Ndessa flank, while the Nigerians made a circuitous march against Mawarenje, to attempt to intercept the enemy in retreat. The flank march to Ndessa was a skilful piece of work through difficult country on compass bearings, and the enemy were completely surprised. They made several efforts to break through the 129th and our Regiment; finding this impossible, they made a hasty retreat on the 21st of September to the south.

On the 22nd No. 2 column was ordered to make a forced

march to Mawarenje, as the enemy in their hasty retreat had bumped into the Nigerians at Bweho. As an instance of the excessive marching on patrol and reconnaissance, "A" Company of the Regiment, under Lieutenant Abraham, marched seventy-two miles in under thirty-six hours in very difficult country. The fighting at Bweho was severe, much of it being hand-to-hand, and the Germans were severely handled. They managed, however, to break through towards the south. In these operations our Regiment had a most difficult night march to Kitandi. There were indeed four days of marching and fighting, with a great shortage of water, the men having none between noon on the 20th of September and the morning of the 24th, except the small amount which each man carried. Even some of this scanty store was given up to assist the horses and mules of the Mountain Battery, the men of the 127th offering to carry or drag the guns when the mules were done in. Captain Lake, with his company, had to make a long night march alone to reinforce the Nigerians. He took part in their successful attack upon Nahungu on the 26th and 27th of September. The main body of the Regiment crossed the Mbemkuru River, remaining there when the rest of the column retired across the river to Nahungu. Here much patrolling work was done with the Ruga-Ruga scouts who were under the command of the well-known Dutch hunter Major Pretorius, D.S.O., M.C. On the 30th of September the Regiment returned to Nahungu. Here Colonel H. Hulseberg took command of his old Regiment. He had been with the 129th since March, 1915. Some days' halt was made at Nahungu, the Nigerians marching off to the east to co-operate with the Lindi force.

On the 9th of October Major Merriman, with two companies of the Regiment and a section of the Mountain Battery, marched towards Nungumboruro, in the hope of cutting off some small enemy patrols. They found that place occupied in some strength. Von Lettow was, in fact, there himself with twelve strong companies. On the 10th Merriman was joined by the rest of the column, at that time consisting only of our Regiment and the Mountain Battery, though the 2nd/3rd King's African Rifles later joined him. All expedients were used to make the enemy believe that he was faced by a considerable force, and on the 13th he evacuated his position. It was a strong and well-prepared one, but von Lettow was aware that turning movements were in progress. The enemy was closely followed up by patrols of the

Regiment in his retreat. An advance was made on Ruangwa on the 16th, and Captain Lake's patrols quickly encountered the enemy, whose position was struck by our advanced guard. The enemy made two unsuccessful counter-attacks before retreating, and Ruangwa was reached in the afternoon of the 16th. On the 18th Mkoe was reached after a sharp fight, which the 55th and the 2nd/3rd King's African Rifles shared with our Regiment. The column reached Mkoe, but afterwards returned to Ruangwa, holding Mkoe only as an outpost to observe the enemy at Mnacho.

Meanwhile, von Lettow had rushed his troops from Nungumboruro through Mnacho to face the Lindi column. There was very severe fighting at Mahiwa with heavy casualties on both sides. It is said that von Lettow put on his full uniform for the first time in the campaign, expecting it to be his last engagement. Once more, however, encirclement failed, and he broke back to the west and succeeded in raiding the camp of the cavalry force near Lukeledi and doing much damage before moving south to Chiwata. Our Regiment, now under Colonel Tanner, who rejoined on the 2nd of November, marched on Lukeledi, which was reached on the night of the 8th of November. Here the Regiment was ordered to march eastwards on Chikukwe. Contact was again established with the enemy at Chiwata. Here the Regiment took up a position known as Baluchi Hill, the enemy being in occupation of Brown Hill. This situation continued until the 14th of November. It was evident, however, that the enemy did not intend to defend Chiwata seriously. The Nigerians were moving down on it from Ndanda in the north, while the Lindi force was clearing the Makende Plateau and pressing in strongly from the east.

The enemy therefore evacuated their position and Chiwata was occupied by the Nigerians and No. 2 column on the 15th. Though von Lettow had slipped away, ninety-eight Germans and four hundred and twenty-five askaris surrendered, and a number of British prisoners were released. All the German guns had been destroyed before the retirement, except one field gun, captured from the Portuguese. This von Lettow took with him in his retirement to Newala. Other German surrenders took place after fighting round Lutshemi.

Tafel's force next demanded attention. It was known that he was moving south to join von Lettow, and on the 20th he was heard of on the Bangalla River. While, therefore, No. 1 column moved towards Newala on the Rovuma, the other forces concentrated on Massassi, our unit moving on the Bangalla River, where they came into contact with a hostile patrol, probably a rear detachment of Tafel's force. On the 26th of November the 129th Baluchis bumped heavily into Tafel's outposts, and had fifty casualties out of a strength of two hundred and fifty. An urgent message had been sent to recall them on news of Tafel's approach, but the Brigade Major "did not decipher the message till the morning when it was too late." This, however, was Tafel's last effort, as on the 28th he surrendered with his whole force. Meanwhile, our Regiment had marched down the Lugo River to within a few miles of the Rovuma, and von Lettow's position at Newala. He, however, made no attempt to stand here, crossing the Rovuma into Portuguese East Africa. The Portuguese troops did nothing to stop him: in fact, they proved a ready source for replenishment of his arms and ammunition. It was also believed that more energetic action by the South African mounted columns might have produced better results.

Von Lettow had, however, only two thousand men left, and, though he was to maintain himself gallantly for another year, and even to march into British territory, he could safely be left to be dealt with by the now considerable force of African troops. It had been decided on the 17th of November that all the Indian troops could safely, and ought to, be withdrawn from Africa before the rainy season, and they were accordingly returned, with the exception of two mountain batteries.

The three Baluch Regiments had nobly maintained their old reputations, and the conduct of the Pathans in very trying circumstances had proved exemplary.

Our Regiment began its eastward march on the 2nd December. Mtama was reached on the 11th of December, where a camp was formed until the 3rd of January. Heavy rain was already beginning, but it could now be regarded with equanimity. Lindi was reached by road on the 10th of January. The Regiment sailed thence to Dar es Salaam. Here the Regiment remained until the 13th of February, when they embarked for India, Karachi being reached on the 21st of February. Although the Regiment had not been engaged in any very serious fighting in Africa, their difficulties may be judged from the number of sick, some eight hundred of all ranks, evacuated as sick, mostly due to fever.

The Regiment at once moved to Quetta for rest and reorganization. In the month of its arrival in India a second battalion was formed which was worthily to represent the Regiment in the successful operations in Palestine culminating in the crowning victory of Megiddo.

In May, 1918, the composition of the Regiment was as follows:

"A" Company.—Baluchis, Brahuis, Transfrontier Pathans.

"B" Company.—Punjabi Musulmans.

"C" Company.—Half-company Mohmands, half-company Punjabi Musulmans.

"D" Company.—Half-company Yusufzais, half-company Punjabi Musulmans.

The time was one of considerable anxiety in India. The long continuance of the war and its extension on many fronts necessitated the raising of many new units and greatly increased the strain on recruiting resources, the best of which had been sucked dry. There was grave political and revolutionary unrest in India. A revolution in Afghanistan had removed the ruler who had stood loyally by his pledges to the British Government; troublesome elements on the frontier had been excited both by religious sympathy with the Turks and by the opportunities afforded by the absence on foreign service of the officers and regiments best qualified to keep them in order. Nevertheless, our Regiment was again warned, in July, 1918, that it would be required for further service overseas.

CHAPTER SEVEN

1918—1929

THE Regiment, under the command of Lieutenant-Colonel H. Hulseberg, D.S.O., with Major E. A. W. Lake as Second-in-Command, left Quetta in September, 1918, seven months after its return from East Africa, and sailed from Karachi on the 13th of October to join the Bushire Field Force. During its short period of training and re-equipment in Quetta it received a new influx of officers from the Western Front, among whom were Captains J. S. Harvey and J. R. James, both later to become Commandants of the Battalion. It may be observed here, also, that among the junior officers accompanying the Battalion was Captain G. Prior, who later joined the South Persian Rifles, thereby laying the foundations of his subsequent spectacular career in the Persian Gulf; in the Second World War he, as Sir Geoffrey Prior, became the Middle East authority on Persian political affairs.

The circumstances which led to our Regiment being summoned to the Persian Gulf were these. The whole of Persia had almost from the outset of the war become an area for the intrigues of German and Turkish agents. These were especially dangerous in the south, where arms and emissaries could readily be passed through to cause trouble in Afghanistan and on the Indian frontier, while threats to Bushire in the Gulf were likely to relieve the pressure on the Turks in Mesopotamia. The only disciplined force in the country, the gendarmerie, trained and commanded by Swedish officers, nearly all of whom were pro-German in their sympathies, was in a state of mutiny and was readily influenced by German agents, particularly the notorious Wassmuss. This man also induced tribes such as the Tangistanis to take up arms against the British and others, like the Kashgais, to assume a hostile attitude.

In consequence of this, the 124th, our present 1st Battalion, was sent to Bushire in March, 1916. At the end of April the Right Wing of this regiment was moved to Bundar Abbas, to form the principal portion of a small force which it was determined to send, under the political control of Sir Percy Sykes, into the interior of Persia. The reason for this dangerous undertaking was the damage that was being done by small bands organized by Germans and Turks which were wandering about South Persia, stirring up the tribesmen, seizing British consuls and generally damaging British prestige and trade. Although Persia was a neutral country whose Government's attitude to the Allied cause was dubious, Sir Percy Sykes hoped to be able to raise a force of Persians, trained by British officers and non-commissioned officers, which would maintain order in South Persia. In this way the risky experiment of the South Persian Rifles was begun. It is beyond our scope to tell of the uniformly excellent services of the wing of the 124th, or to follow their ceaseless marches and expeditions. In August, 1917, it was determined to increase the Right Wing to a full battalion, to be called the 3rd/124th, as another battalion had been formed from the Left Wing of the Regiment, and had already greatly distinguished itself as the 2nd/124th in Mesopotamia. The increase was effected by the raising in India of a new wing, partly from volunteers from the labour battalions, and partly by obtaining raw recruits from the Baluch hill tribes. On the 1st of May, 1918, this new wing joined the old one near Shiraz, and the 3rd/124th was fully constituted. The G.S.O.1 of Sir Percy Sykes's force was, it may be noted, Lieutenant-Colonel G. P. Grant, who had led the detachment of our Regiment at the capture of Nodiz Fort in 1901.

By this time, however, the situation around Shiraz had rapidly deteriorated. The collapse of the Russian Army and the apparently overwhelming success of the Germans on the Western Front in March and April, 1918, had convinced the Persian Government, as well as the tribesmen, that the British were going to lose the war. The South Persian Rifles were also obviously untrustworthy. In spite, therefore, of a successful action at Deh Shaikh on the 25th of May, the garrison of Shiraz found themselves besieged during the summer of 1918, most of the South Persian Rifles having mutinied or deserted. Fears of another Kut and the consequent blow to British prestige dangerously near to Afghanistan led to an urgent call for assistance. The Indian Government was asked to send strong reinforcements to Bushire, in order to relieve Shiraz. This call was the reason for the warning given to our Regiment in July. Action from Bushire was, however, impossible at the time owing to want of men, the severe heat at Bushire, and the occupation of the difficult and roadless passes between that port and Shiraz by great numbers of tribesmen. By the autumn matters had greatly improved owing to the collapse of Germany and Turkey, and the arrest of Wassmuss and of other disturbing elements. The tribesmen had also got tired of sitting round Shiraz and had returned to their grazing grounds. The influenza epidemic had indeed caused the deaths of some eighteen per cent. of the force at Shiraz, the 3rd/124th alone losing more than a hundred and seventy men; but it had at least equally affected the civil population and the hostile tribesmen.

Our Regiment arrived at Bushire on the 18th of November, 1918, and immediately marched the fifty-five miles to Daliki to join the striking force under Brigadier-General Elmslie. It was at once employed in picqueting the hills for the protection of convoys, and in road making. The first contact with the enemy was made on the 30th of November, when the picquets were attacked in the Fili-Fili Pass. The enemy were driven off with a loss to the Regiment of six men killed. This work continued until the 20th of December, when the striking force attacked the Kamarij Pass, held by a small but determined band of tribesmen, who were described as rebels. Our Regiment, with one section of a mountain battery, formed the left column of the attack. The men had to climb up the steep height of the Tang-i-Malu, or Pass of the Old Woman, seven thousand four hundred feet high, descend three thousand feet, and then climb the still-steeper Tang-i-Dukhtar, the Pass of the Daughter: no mean task in mid-winter. The heights were successfully cleared and junction made with the 55th Coke's Rifles in Kamarij village. Leaving the 55th to hold the village, the Regiment returned to its camp very late in the afternoon. The next few weeks were spent in the arduous task of making a passable road over the defiles. The Regiment moved to the summit of the pass on the 30th of December. On the 26th of January, 1919, it marched to Rahdar and joined the headquarters of the striking force. On the 28th it marched to Kazarun, where a detachment of the Shiraz force was met. The Regiment remained at Kazarun until the 7th of April, employed in the endless work of road making, and in preparing a strong position. The more settled conditions now prevailing made it possible for the striking force to be broken up. The Regiment, with a squadron of the 15th Lancers, marched on Shiraz on the 8th of April, the first day's march of eighteen miles in sleet and snow being described as particularly trying. On the 11th of April the Regiment reached Shiraz, in relief of the 3rd/124th, which left for India. The Regiment remained at Shiraz until March, 1920, when orders came for the return of all Indian troops, with the exception of small consular guards, to their own country.

By this time the South Persian Rifles were a well-disciplined force, and there was no further need to keep the Indian troops in the country. Our Regiment therefore left Shiraz on the 21st and 22nd of March, 1920, and marched to Borazjun. A railway line had been laid to this place from Bushire, and by this the Regiment travelled for the last forty-five miles of its journey. On the 17th of April the Regiment embarked at Bushire, and on the 21st reached Karachi. Here it remained until the 20th of May, when it entrained for Multan.

Thus our service in the First World War ended. Opportunities for distinction and casualties had mostly occurred through the drafts supplied to other battalions. Nevertheless, the Battalion had served with credit on three fronts, and had endured much hardship with its traditional cheerfulness.

The extent of the services of individual members of the Regiment, whether serving with it or with other units, may be judged from the number of medals awarded. This was as follows:

1914 Star	253
1914-15 Star	476
British War Medal	2,284
North-West Frontier Indian General Service Medal, 1919	212
General Service Medal, Persia, 1918-19	1,196

This may be a suitable point at which to refer to the campaign and battle honours of the First World War awarded in 1926 to the Regiment and the battalions with which in 1922 it had been grouped. These honours numbered twenty-two, of which ten were selected to be borne on colours or appointments. These twenty-two distinctions had been earned on seven different fronts. In addition, the distinction of "Afghanistan, 1919," had been won for the Baluch Regiment by the 1st and 3rd Battalions of the 124th.

A great reorganization of the Indian Army now took place. The amalgamation of battalions in one group or regiment was a change necessitated by the defects which the First World War had exposed, especially the difficulty of finding reinforcements of officers and men for battalions suffering heavy casualties on service. It also facilitated training of recruits on a uniform system by making one of the battalions a purely training one. It also equalized the chances of regimental promotion. These advantages must be held to outweigh a certain loss of individuality involved in the pooling of distinctions and traditions.

The chief architect of this far-reaching reform was General (later Field-Marshal) Sir Claud Jacob, who had risen from being Adjutant of the 3rd Beloochees to Chief of the General Staff, India, after holding one of the highest field appointments in France. The depot system, whereby each unit going on active service jettisoned its recruits, its sick, its families, records and heavy baggage in any convenient cantonment in India, had broken down under the strain of a prolonged world war. The officers, on whom not only the successful training of reinforcements but the maintenance of records and accounts depended, were being constantly changed, with the result that there was little continuity in either training or documentation.

The 10th Baluch Regiment was happy in its grouping. Three of the battalions, the 127th, 129th and 130th, had always been closely inter-related. The 124th and 126th, if more recent in their connection, were formed of the same material. The 10th or Training Battalion of the group was the 2nd Battalion of the 124th, a unit which had greatly distinguished itself in Mesopotamia and Palestine. Its survival was in itself a compliment, as only twelve out of all the numerous new battalions raised during the war remained in the reorganized Indian Army, while many of the old regiments of the line were disbanded. This fate was naturally inevitable for the other new battalions connected with the Baluch Regiments: the 2nd Battalions of the 127th, 129th and 130th, and the 3rd Battalion of the 124th. With the exception of the 2nd/130th, these had all seen service overseas.

We may now return to the history of our Battalion, the 3rd Battalion (Queen Mary's Own) 10th Baluch Regiment, its new name. Immediately after its arrival in Multan the whole Battalion was given two months' war leave. The season was not, however, one of rest and quiet. It was the time of the Khilafat agitation, when the feelings of the Mohammedan sepoys were skilfully worked upon by political agitators. It was the period of the "Hijrat," when the unfortunate Musulman cultivators were deluded into selling their land and belongings and emigrating into the Islamic land of Afghanistan, where plenty was supposed to await them. Their sufferings and disillusionment particularly affected the Mohmand and Baluch sepoys of the Regiment. There were other sources of discontent: high prices, bad rations and rumours that the Government would not fulfil its promises to better the lot of the sepoy. It says much for the work of the officers and the discipline of the Regiment that this difficult time was successfully overcome.

The Battalion was not long left in the quiet of Multan. On the 21st of December, 1920, it moved to Chaman and quitted that place for Loralai at the end of March, 1921. In February of that year the gratifying announcement was received that Her Majesty Queen Mary was to be shown in the Army List as Colonel-in-Chief of the Regiment. This continued only until October, 1924, when, on His Majesty King George V becoming Colonel-in-Chief of the 10th Baluch Regiment, Her Majesty Queen Mary relinquished the Colonelcy-in-Chief of our Battalion, which, however, proudly continued to hold the title "Queen Mary's Own."

It was at this time that Lieutenant-Colonel A. E. Stewart, M.C., assumed command of the Battalion. Originally in the Black Watch, he had served in the Boer War with the Argyll and Sutherland Highlanders, and later joined the 124th (Duchess of Connaught's Own) Baluchistan Infantry, with whom he had done all his Indian regimental soldiering. It was fortunate for the Battalion that it was during his tenure the smooth but complicated amalgamation of the various battalions into a regiment with an identical outlook took place. A born administrator, with a flair for sound and simple organization, he soon had his hands full of work of the most intricate and difficult nature. Owing to faulty administration in the Depot and lack of adequate supervision by experienced regular officers, mostly absent on service, the accounts, records, documentation and general interior economy were in a condition which would have appalled a less strong character. The Battalion was fortunate that Stewart had been selected to clean up this Augean stable. With the assistance of his newly appointed Second-in-Command, Major A. S. Auret, his Adjutant, J. R. James, and his company commanders, J. S. Harvey and A. C. Taylor, he tackled the job with an energy and force which have now made part of our history.

Faced with an unintelligible mass of accounts, badly kept, rarely inspected and woefully lacking in even the elementary principles of book-keeping, with an accumulation of unsettled claims and a mass of unanswered correspondence from the audit authorities (who were in a similar mess), his action was characteristic. Having ensured that none of the men's interests was jeopardized, he merely drew a formidable red line across the appropriate column; anything above the line he handed over to the Government to disentangle; for every item below this "Plimsoll mark" he accepted responsibility. Confronted with this empirical gesture, the Military Accounts Department at first reacted violently, later demurred, and finally capitulated gracefully when Stewart, armed with all his facts, made a personal appearance. Thereafter, under the astute and thrifty management of this formidable Scot, the regimental accounts grew and prospered.

Stewart, now Colonel of the Battalion, and Fowler, whom he succeeded in that honourable office, had many similar traits of character, not the least of which was the respect, amounting sometimes to terror, with which they inspired their subordinates. Their barks were, however, far worse than their bites. Tireless in his pursuit of efficiency, adamant against any thing or any person encroaching on regimental tradition, disdainful of "eyewash" or any meretricious aid to attract superior attention, he set an example of regimental fidelity which has been lasting in its effects. His spare time was devoted to sport, small- and big-game shooting and fishing. Any leave he took in India was during the hot weather, when he repaired to the Central Provinces before the monsoon hit the jungles. To encourage his young officers in the healthy pursuit of game, he circulated a holograph pamphlet showing from his own great experience the most interesting and most economical methods of tiger shooting. By chance this pamphlet came to the attention of that other great "shikari" Major-General A. E. Wardrop when the Battalion was in the Lahore district. Wardrop was so impressed by the importance of these notes that he persuaded Stewart to have them published. In due course Longmans produced the book, "Tiger and Other Game," which is now considered one of the few classics on the subject.

The reader will forgive, it is hoped, this digression, which has taken us beyond our chronological order.

On the 4th of July, 1921, the Regiment took over the outposts

Orakzai　　Punjabi Musulman　Mohmand　　　Brahui
TYPES OF THE REGIMENT *circa* 1912

Khattak　　　　Punjabi Musulman　　　　Brahui

Punjabi Musulman　　　　Baluch　　　　　Afridi
TYPES OF THE REGIMENT *circa* 1924

of the Lower Zhob. It was relieved of them at the end of March, 1922, but in the middle of November took them over again until the end of January, 1923, when the charge of the posts was given to the Zhob Levies. In the summer of that year (1923) the Regiment moved to Chaman, where it remained until the end of November, 1924, when it moved to Lahore. The time at Chaman was without incident, the Regiment being at one time employed for three months in digging the new water line to Murda Karez. While at Lahore in 1925 the Battalion had the honour of receiving a beautiful silver cup from Her Majesty Queen Mary.

The years did not pass without changes in the internal constitution of the Battalion. In 1924 it was regimentally decided that each company should contain platoons of the various classes recruited by the Regiment. There were then eight platoons of Punjabi Mohammedans, two each of Brahuis, Baluchis and Khattaks, and one each of Yusufzais and Afridis (Malek Din Khels). In August, 1925, orders were received from Army Headquarters that the "class company" and not the "class platoon" organization should be followed. At the end of 1925 further orders were received that the Baluchis and Brahuis should be replaced by Dogra Brahmans.

The decision to terminate for the second time the recruitment of Baluchis and Brahuis, however regrettable as marking the end of an old story, was inevitable. It was found impossible to get an adequate number of recruits, and many of those obtained were declared by the Training Battalion to be unlikely to make efficient soldiers. Moreover, the dislike of the Baluch for routine discipline and his liability to home-sickness led to numerous desertions.

There had been a platoon of Hill or Dogra Brahmans with the Regiment for two years before August, 1920, when it was transferred to the Kumaon Rifles; but the formation of the Dogra Brahman Company was the first instance of a full Hindu company in the history of the Regiment.

The recruitment of Dogras was a major decision, the policy being laid down by the Adjutant-General with its implementation in the hands of the newly instituted annual conference of commanding officers held in Karachi in November. The outstanding success of this novel departure from Baluch tradition is now common knowledge, being proved on many splendid occasions in the acid test of battle, and it is necessary therefore to record the manner in which the firm foundations were laid. At the conference held in the Baluch Mess in Karachi on the 12th of November, 1925, the proposal was discussed by the following commanding officers:

    Lieutenant-Colonel G. D. R. MacMahon, 1st Battalion.
    Lieutenant-Colonel J. C. Gretton, 2nd Battalion.
    Lieutenant-Colonel A. E. Stewart, M.C., 3rd Battalion.
    Major B. de L. Brock, M.C., 4th Battalion.
    Lieutenant-Colonel H. D. Moore, D.S.O., 5th Battalion.
    Lieutenant-Colonel W. M. MacLeod, 10th Battalion.
    Major S. Van B. Laing, D.S.O., M.C., Recruiting Officer for Dogras.

As Dogra Rajputs were enlisted up to capacity by the regular Dogra units, the choice of classes was restricted to Dogra Brahmans, Jats, Girths and Kannets. Of these the Jats, Girths and Kannets were of doubtful value, as their martial tradition was negligible and their enthusiasm for service faint-hearted. On the other hand, the agricultural Dogra Brahman had proved himself in many Dogra and Punjab regiments as a keen soldier, anxious to serve, and of sturdy physique. To provide one company per active battalion and its reinforcements in the Training Battalion, it was reckoned that almost a thousand men would be required, not too great a demand on this particular class, which the recruiting officer computed had about eight thousand men available. It was therefore decided to ask Army Headquarters to transfer from other units a Dogra Brahman nucleus for each battalion of two Indian officers, two havildars, four naiks, eight lance-naiks and forty-four other ranks. The recruitment was from the Kangra and Hoshiarpur districts, later extended to Jammu and Poonch.

In the following spring Colonel Stewart toured Hoshiarpur and Kangra and met with a splendid reception in all recruiting areas. In the following three years the "baby" "C" Company of Dogra Brahmans grew to manhood and a strength of a hundred and thirty under the paternal solicitude of its commander, Major F. B. G. Wetherall, M.C.

The Battalion was stationed in Lahore Cantonments from November, 1924, to February, 1929, a period of hard training during the delightful Punjab winters and those ferocious hot weathers for which Kipling made Mian Mir famous. As the men enjoyed in alternate years three months' furlough or two months' leave and the officers had two months' leave annually, or long

THE OFFICERS, 1924

Back row—Captain L. White, Lieutenant G. R. Moriarty, Captain W. E. Maxwell, Lieutenant E. K. Tarver, Lieutenant W. King, Captain C. J. Dyer.
Front row—Major F. B. G. Wetherall, M.C., Major A. S. Auret, Lieutenant-Colonel A. E. Stewart, M.C., Major E. A. W. Lake, Captain A. C. Taylor, D.S.O.

leave home every three years, the rigours of the summer months were agreeably mitigated for all ranks.

The practice of keeping retired and absent officers in touch with Battalion affairs by means of a quarterly Adjutant's Letter had been instituted. A few extracts from these letters will present an ingenuous picture of regimental activity with its colours intact:

LETTER DATED 21ST JANUARY, 1927

"The outstanding event of the quarter ending 31st Dec. was the visit to Lahore of H.E. Lord Irwin, the new Viceroy, during October.

"As there are only two infantry battalions in Lahore there was plenty of work during this period. The Khattaks gave a dance Tamasha before Their Excellencies at Government House, which appealed particularly to Lady Irwin. 'B' Company gave a Mobilization demonstration at a garden party in Cantonments. We supplied several Guards of Honour and lined miles of streets.

"Letter from the Military Secretary to the Viceroy to the G.O.C. Lahore District:'Will you please convey His Excellency's thanks to the officers and men of the 10th Baluchis for their Khattak dance on Tuesday evening and for the most interesting and instructive display they gave yesterday afternoon. From what he saw on these occasions and from their Guard of Honour and the Guard at Government House, it is quite obvious that they are a very fine regiment.'

"Colonel Stewart arrived from home leave on 6th December with some notable presents for the Mess:

"1. A signed photograph from Queen Mary, beautifully framed and now occupying a position of honour in the Mess.

"2. A silver salver from General Fowler, C.B., D.S.O., in recognition of his appointment as Colonel of the Battalion.

"3. A silver replica of a sepoy bomber—a beautiful model presented by certain officers who served with the Battalion in the Great War.

"4. A silver bowl (a Scottish 'methar' cup) presented by Colonel Stewart.

*"*TRAINING. *Platoon and Company training continued hard during October and November. The Machine Gun Platoon attended a Concentration Camp at Hoshiarpore in Dec. The Battalion was in camp at Niaz Beg about 11 miles from Lahore*

from 5th to 19th December for battalion training. The progress made by N.C.Os. and the regiment's ability to conceal itself from aircraft were the most noticeable features.

"This was shown on a Brigade Field Day when the battalion did an approach march of over $7\frac{1}{2}$ miles in two hours. Enemy cavalry, armoured cars and three aeroplanes were scouring the country for us, but we managed to arrive within 800 yards without being detected."

Our principal role in Lahore was internal security duties. How these duties were carried out can be seen from this extract from the Adjutant's Letter of July, 1927:

"The outstanding event of the last quarter was our participation in the Lahore Riots of May 3rd—8th. Communal tension between the Sikhs and the Muhammadans in the Punjab had been becoming gradually more acute. Lahore itself had been comparatively free from this modern development in Indian politics, but this was too good to last. On 3rd May a slight incident occurred which led to the murder of four Muhammadans by a crowd of Sikhs that night.

"The funeral next day accentuated the bitter feelings, and before nightfall murder and assault were rampant. The troops were then called out. Our first company—'D' under Captain A. C. Taylor, D.S.O.—reached the city at 6 p.m. on the 4th and was immediately dispersed in all directions in patrols and picquets. The next company, under Lieut. E. K. Tarver, followed at 8.30 p.m. and was also swallowed up in the alleyways of Lahore. Next morning the last remaining company and Battalion H.Qs. moved to the city.

"A peculiar feature of this rioting was its absence of any anti-government expression. It consisted of short and sharp isolated affrays between the two sects, and the assailants always disappeared with unforgivable agility on the arrival of police or troops. All troops had orders to open fire without warning on any persons caught committing assaults or arson. This sanction had not to be utilised. After five days the troops were gradually withdrawn and our last company returned to cantonment on the 17th May."

. . . .

"OFFICERS. Major A. S. Auret has been promoted Lieutenant-Colonel from 24th May. He was also awarded the O.B.E. in the last Birthday Honours.

"TRAINING. *The musketry results for so far have been better than last year, and we hope to be very near the top of the Lahore District averages this year.*

"Our Lines are in a lamentable condition owing to the fact that Government has decided after a delay of 29 years to rebuild them. The accumulation of debris excites every passing sandstorm to do its damnedest, and the men suffer in consequence."

In July, 1927, Lieutenant-Colonel A. S. Auret became Commandant. As he and his predecessor had been working hand in glove for the past five years, the transition was painless except for the parting with Stewart, who had rehabilitated the Battalion into a first-class unit. The musketry returns for that year were the highest since the war, and the signallers' figure of merit was 98.6, also the highest. In November, 1928, the Battalion earned great commendation in the large-scale Northern Command manœuvres. Two features, often noticeable in the history of the Regiment, wonderful mobility and unfailing cheeriness, were stated to be "the admiration of all who had the pleasure of working with them." In the absence of Colonel Auret, the Battalion was commanded for the manœuvres by the Second-in-Command, Major M. L. A. Gompertz, who had been appointed such the previous year. His invention of suitable equipment to be carried on the platoon Lewis-gun mule to provide the men with hot tea was a very pleasant aid in trouble, and was later adopted by many other regiments.

After some false alarms and postponements, the Battalion left Lahore on the 12th of February, 1929, for Waziristan. Marching from Bannu, it reached Razani, its new station, on the 20th of February.

CHAPTER EIGHT

1929—1940

DURING the ten remaining years of peace preceding the Second World War the Regiment carried on its characteristic activities in all parts of the Indian Empire: from Wana in Waziristan to Bassein in Burma, and from St. Thomas's Mount, Madras, to Alexander Ridge, Razmak.

Shortly after its arrival in Razani the Battalion was reorganized on the new imperial scale of H.Q. Company, three rifle companies and one machine-gun company armed with six Vickers guns (peace strength, seven hundred and twenty-eight; war strength, seven hundred and eight). In May, 1929, the Brass Band, which had existed since 1877, was abolished. This sad decision, agreed to by all officers with only two dissentients, was imposed by considerations of efficiency; the establishment provided for sixteen stretcher-bearers, employed as musicians, the remaining twenty bandsmen being borne on rifle-company strength but normally unavailable for duties. In the harsh conditions of a frontier garrison, where "nights in bed" were one in two, this burden on company requirements was intolerable. On a star-lit night in May the Bandmaster, Havildar Astora Khan, himself the son of a former bandmaster in the Battalion, gave his final performance. As the bandsmen's pensions, transfers to other units and general interests had been carefully safeguarded by Lieutenant-Colonel Auret, the occasion was marked by more cordiality and good cheer than such a break with a fifty-two-year association could warrant, if the necessity had not been understood and appreciated by all.

With Auret as Commandant the Battalion was fortunate and happy. Having spent a considerable time as a junior officer with the Zhob Militia and carried out perilous expeditions in the vague hinterlands between Afghanistan, Persia and India, his knowledge and experience of the frontier and the tribesmen were extensive and thorough. In his hands the Battalion soon found its feet on the precipitous slopes surrounding the now-abandoned post of Razani. The new tactics, necessitated by the changed organization and armament, made battalion and brigade exercises exciting and valuable under his keen tactical eye. An intelligent instructor, he made even the dullest paragraph in Field Service Regulations interesting and informative. He exploited the junior officers' keenness on horsemanship by making them use their horses in all training, setting an example himself on his well-bred charger, "Ulster." Similarly to increase the men's mobility, he had the Battalion equipped with *chaplis* and footless hose, a form of footwear to be universally adopted later by all regular battalions on the frontier.

The principles of mobility and surprise thus engendered were suddenly brought into active play. During this year Afghanistan was in the throes of revolution and widespread fighting in which the Wazirs of Waziristan took full share. At the end of October the Government of India decided to reoccupy Wano (now Wana), abandoned during the Afghan War of 1919. On the 30th of October the Battalion was ordered to move by motor transport to Manzai. There a column, under the command of Major-General R. C. Wilson, was formed consisting of a detachment, 2nd Armoured Car Company (Royal Tank Corps), 17th Mountain Battery, 9th Field Company Sappers and Miners, 3rd/1st Punjab Regiment, and 1st and 3rd Battalions 10th Baluch Regiment. The expedition was on light scale, speed and surprise being the main essentials for success. On the 12th of November the column marched into Wano. Not a shot was fired during the long march up via Jandola, Sarwakai and Dargai Oba. The local Wazirs, still looting in Kabul, were outmanœuvred and, on their return to the Wana Plain, accepted the occupation force with good enough grace.

Then followed a period of privation and sheer hard toil. Wana, the site of an old Militia fort, is a flat, stony plain, not unlike Quetta in miniature, four thousand five hundred feet above sea-level and only fifteen miles from the Durand Line. The camp was constructed on the usual frontier model, a mud-and-stone perimeter, two aprons of wire, picquet posts and cramped dug-down billets of mud walls with tent roofs. These, later under the craftsmanship of Brevet Lieutenant-Colonel Gompertz, became Wana huts of a durable and comfortable construction.

No outstanding event occurred during the following year except the departure of Lieutenant-Colonel A. S. Auret in February, 1931, after his four-year tenure of command. He was the last 127th Baluch officer of pre-1914 service, and his leave-taking evoked from all ranks a remarkable demonstration of their affection, the men lining the roadside for a mile from the camp, with many of his old friends among the Indian officers and non-commissioned officers showing marked emotion. Lieutenant-Colonel M. L. A. Gompertz now assumed command, with Major J. F. Meiklejohn, who had transferred from the Poona Horse in 1929, as Second-in-Command. This transference of officers of suitable seniority between all regiments of the Indian Army was becoming increasingly common about this period. It is of interest to record that at the annual conference of the 10th Baluch Regiment in Karachi in 1931 four of the battalion commanders (E. A. W. Lake, A. S. Auret, R. D. Davies and P. Quayle) were 127th officers.

Gompertz, another sound administrator, soon had his administrative capacity taxed. Leaving Wana in February, 1931, the Battalion arrived in its new station, Secunderabad, exactly a month later. A halt of over a fortnight at Jhelum gave the new Commanding Officer an opportunity of arranging a complicated leave programme so that as many men as possible should at least visit their homes. Leave and furlough had been severely restricted in Wana, and railway fares from distant Secunderabad were certain to be a great hardship for men called home on private business. The short interlude at Jhelum also gave an opportunity to show the local inhabitants—Jhelum being a most important Baluch recruiting area—the stuff they produced. We read that the Dhol and Surnai Band, the substitute for the Brass Band and lately officially recognized by Army Headquarters, performed at a district tea party, the bandsmen wearing for the first time their ceremonial dress, green *safa*, silver-buttoned khaki tunic, cherry trousers, and white gaiters.

For the uninitiated it might be explained that the *surnai* is a reed pipe capable of producing music of a timbre usually associated with a bagpipe. It is, however, a native instrument, indigenous to the North-West of India, and the skilled musician, instead of using a windbag, fills his cheeks with the requisite bellow power. Inexpert performers can rarely control this pressure and therefore fail to produce music with either harmony or modulation. Fortunately the Battalion had three Scots, Meiklejohn, Harvey and Sime, who understood this type of music and supervised the training of the Band. The result was a Dhol and Surnai Band which later—on many an arduous undertaking—was to uplift the spirit and banish fatigue with its merry interpretation of Highland marches. For the sepoys' concerts it was an unfailing delight, as the musicians, mostly Mirassis, thrived on entertainment and, being professionals, were versatile and catholic in their erudition.

Secunderabad, situated in what was termed the "sloth-belt" of India, was not popular with officers or men. Consequently, an order to mobilize, received on the 22nd of May at 2 a.m., was greeted with satisfaction, despite the ungodly hour. With a rapidity comparable only with Fowler's mobilization for Somaliland in 1909, Gompertz reported his Battalion ready for war on the 28th of May. It was not until almost a month later that the Battalion embarked for Calcutta in s.s. *Egra* for Rangoon. This venerable craft provoked the oldest member of the Battalion, the great mess abdar, Abdul Ghani, to observe that she was not as steady as the ship in which he sailed to Somaliland thirty years before.

The Battalion arrived at Rangoon on the 22nd of June, 1931, and was at once transferred to the Rangoon Brigade. Colonel Gompertz was appointed to the military command of the Irrawaddy Civil Division, an area over two hundred miles long and from forty to a hundred miles broad, mostly low-lying delta country, comprising five civil districts.

It was found that, though the southern part of the division was well in hand, the northern part, and in particular the Henzada district, was in a state of active and successful rebellion. In Henzada the rebels not only terrorized the countryside by murders and dacoities, but sacked the police outposts, killing many of the police and taking their arms. The police themselves were overworked and entirely insufficient in number.

There were only six British officers with the Battalion at the outset, so that the Adjutant and the Quartermaster had often to go out in charge of small columns. Colonel Gompertz was given a free hand in the disposal of the troops and established a system of platoon posts, each post commanding an area, generally a township, the equivalent of the Indian *tahsil*. The platoon commanders thus worked independently, in touch with the civil and police officials, and there was much scope for the junior officers to show initiative and judgment. The situation was, in fact, singularly like that which the Regiment had had to deal with nearly fifty years before in Upper Burma. The resemblance included the creation of a Mounted Infantry company formed by Subadar-Major Ahmad Khan from the mule drivers of the Battalion and commanded by him: his work in harrying the rebel leaders earned for him the Indian Distinguished Service Medal. There was, however, one feature which made the work of the Battalion even more arduous than it had been in 1887. In the delta districts the Irrawaddy River runs in the rains at a level higher than that of the surrounding countryside, being retained in its course only by high *bunds*. During the rainy months, therefore, no drainage is possible and the rain-water remains until the monsoon finishes and the river falls to a lower level. In 1931 the rainfall was far above the average, the river rising to within two inches of the highest level ever recorded. The country thus became a marsh, in which neither wheel nor animal could move, even in those parts which were not out of a man's depth. These conditions persisted until the end of October.

The nature of the work during the rainy months may be illustrated by two examples. In August a concentric raid on several villages of the Henzada district was carried out by five platoons of the Battalion and a platoon of Military Police, each platoon working separately and secretly. On this occasion, as on many others, it rained almost without a break throughout the operation. One platoon of "A" Company, under Subadar Sher Zaman, marched thirty miles between 9 p.m. and 3 p.m. of the next day, over flooded rice fields, knee-deep in mud and water, and along unmetalled tracks deep in mud. Another platoon, which the Adjutant, Captain Moriarty, accompanied, had to march seven miles through waist-deep water on a pitch-black night. The marching depth ahead was gauged by the visibility or otherwise of the guide, a small but stout-hearted Burmese sub-inspector of police. Provided that his head remained above water, the column continued. When, however, Captain Moriarty saw with his electric torch only bubbles and a floating hat, the column halted, rescued the guide, and made a detour to find less deep water.

In September during a raid carried out by Captain Dalton and Lieutenant Nicoll with two platoons, the operation had to be carried out in sampans or native boats. When the village which was the objective was surrounded at dawn, the work was carried on in breast-deep water.

As the rebels grew more chary of encounters, the ambush was adopted as the most effective weapon, sometimes with troops disguised as Indian settlers, sometimes with waterborne operations on Q-boat lines. For his continued good leadership in this work, and for his personal gallantry at Hneggyo, Lieutenant R. C. B. Waller was given the Military Cross. (This gallant and able officer, after distinguished service in the Middle East in the Second World War, rose rapidly to the rank of Lieutenant-Colonel. On his way from Simla in 1943 to take up an appointment with the Allied Military Headquarters in Washington, he was murdered by a bandit in the Kalka rail-motor. The Battalion and the whole Baluch Regiment thus lost one of their finest officers.)

From November onwards, as the countryside dried up, quicker movement and the use of animals and wheels allowed of more effective harrying of the rebel gangs. The police force was re-organized and strengthened, and the villagers recovered their confidence. The remaining dacoits were hunted down, or were driven into other districts where, being friendless, they were quickly caught. By the end of January it was possible to reduce the number of outposts, and to send to India first "B" and later "D" Company to enjoy long-overdue leave and furlough. The remainder of the Regiment sailed from Burma for India on the 25th of March, 1932.

Throughout these operations the men of the Regiment displayed those qualities of initiative, mobility and cheerfulness which had marked it in so many previous campaigns. Most cordial relations had been established with the Burma Police, a permanent memorial to which exists in the very handsome silver Lamaing Bowl presented to the Battalion by the officers and men of the Burma Police serving in the Bassein, Maubin and Henzada districts. On the silver panels of the bowl are depicted three episodes of the Battalion's work during the rebellion.

The farewell order to the Regiment of the Officer Commanding the Rangoon Area was couched in the highest terms.

When the Battalion returned to Secunderabad it had been, with the exception of ten weeks in 1931, on field service, or under field service conditions, for three years on end. For their services during these arduous years the majority of the Battalion earned the Indian General Service Medal with bars for Waziristan, 1930-31, and Burma, 1931-32. Much reorganization and overhaul of equipment was necessary.

In December, 1933, Lieutenant-Colonel J. F. Meiklejohn succeeded Lieutenant-Colonel Gompertz (whose tenure was cut short on promotion to the Kohat District Staff) in the command of the Battalion. During his period of command Gompertz rendered signal service to the Battalion by instituting a men's provident fund. This was carried out in the teeth of much opposition, but soon fully justified itself and was copied by other units. The remainder of the Battalion's stay at Secunderabad was uneventful, its pleasantness being enhanced by the fact that the Acting Resident at Hyderabad was Lieutenant-Colonel J. C. Tate, an old officer of the Battalion.

On the 27th of September, 1934, the Battalion arrived at St. Thomas's Mount, Madras, thus completing its circumambulation of the principal Indian cities from farthest north to the most extreme south; one company was stationed at Trichinopoly.

Although the officers of the Battalion received unstinted hospitality in Madras, it was an expensive station both for officers and men. The absence of opportunity to train with other arms, and the lack of suitable ground, made it a difficult station in which to maintain efficiency. The Battalion therefore welcomed the opportunity to participate in the district concentration at Bangalore in January, 1936. In view of the difficulties involved, it was the more creditable that the remarks of inspecting officers should have continued to be so uniformly favourable. It is only necessary to quote those of the Commander-in-Chief, Sir Philip Chetwode, in January, 1935: "I inspected the 3rd/10th Baluchis under Colonel Meiklejohn. They gave me the impression of being as smart and well-turned-out a regiment as any in the Indian Army, a particularly fine-looking lot of men. I noticed that their mules were considerably above the average, and were particularly well looked after."

The barracks in Madras were originally built for the Madras Elephant Artillery and were in fact three separate forts. It is peculiar to note with what persistency the Battalion's footsteps were dogged by indifferent habitations throughout its history, and these, combined with atrocious training facilities, made a dim prospect for Meiklejohn, who by this time had become more Baluch than the Baluchis themselves. The war block scheme, devised to thin out the growing list of majors in the Indian Army, and its consequent reshuffling of officers between units, cost the Battalion the loss of Major A. W. H. Sime, D.S.O., M.C. (who had been awarded a brevet majority for his services in Burma), and Captain D. F. Dalton, both transferred. In 1936 Subadar-Major and Honorary Lieutenant Ahmed Khan, Bahadur, I.D.S.M., retired. He had exchanged from Indian Cavalry after the First World War, and had proved himself on many an occasion a first-class infantryman and an Indian officer of the greatest integrity and resource. He was succeeded by Subadar-Major Fazal Khan, who held that high office until 1941.

Although the appointment of subadar-majors is based entirely on merit, the promotion of another Punjabi Musulman, the fourth in succession, shows how esteemed and important a position this class held in the Regiment. Since 1844 the Punjabi Musulmans had been regularly, and at times irregularly, recruited and now composed half the Battalion strength. Their valour, steadfastness and loyalty had been proved on many a field. In the First World War the Punjab had contributed as volunteers the majority of the whole Indian Army, and the Baluch connection with its various recruiting areas had remained strong and intimate. At the 1936 conference in Karachi it was decided to make recruitment from the several Punjab districts on a percentage basis, as follows:

Rawalpindi	35 per cent.
Jhelum	35 per cent.
Gujrat, Shahpur, Attock and Mianwali	30 per cent.

With all the fluctuations and changes in recruitment policy in peace, vastly extended and variegated as it became under the stress of the Second World War, the Punjab remained the backbone of the Baluch Regiment and a never-failing source of splendid soldiers from, literally, generation to generation.

In November, 1937, the Battalion set sail from Madras to Karachi, calling at Colombo and Bombay. It was a cheerful voyage. Karachi, the home of the Regiment, was a pleasant change from South India, and the officers were overwhelmed by the hospitality shown them by its generous inhabitants. The commodious new Baluch Mess, shared with the Training Battalion, was a fitting venue to return this hospitality, and was often the scene of many a gay party. Karachi at this period was a two-year station, but very soon orders arrived for the Battalion to move to

Razmak, Waziristan, within the year, a rather unkind cut, particularly for the men who had soldiered so many thousand miles from their homes since 1929 and were, naturally enough, looking forward to two years' peaceful conditions.

In December, 1937, Lieutenant-Colonel J. S. Harvey took over command from Meiklejohn, appointed Commandant of the Physical Training Schools, India. Harvey, a staunch Scot imbued with the fervid loquacity of a race which produced Burns and Scott, was a demon for work, for training and for the Battalion's good name. Having served under Winston Churchill in France and Stewart in Chaman, his military outlook was inevitably stamped with the personal touch in all affairs, often explosive. There was no regimental activity into which he did not hurl his well-trained body and soul.

In the spring of 1938 battalion and brigade training was carried out in Kotri, Sind. It will interest readers brought up to swifter methods that in those days movement by road in motor transport was rigorously limited to a hundred miles per diem. The advance party to Kotri had consumed this allowance by 3 p.m. of their second day's movement. They were in sight and walking distance of their objective, but had to spend the night in the desert, anchored by regulations. Training was concentrated on mountain warfare in preparation for the move to Razmak. Razmak, on its six-thousand-foot Waziristan plateau, situated squarely between the warring tribes of Wazirs and Mahsuds, with a garrison of five Indian battalions and one British regiment, its famous Indian mountain batteries and its equally famous Indian Sappers, had grown since the early 1920's into the most efficient *corps d'élite* in the Army in India. Harvey was determined that our Battalion should take a fitting place in this proud company, and worked the men hard to this end.

In August the tactical advance party under Major A. C. Taylor went to Razmak for its three months' training which ensured a smooth tactical and administrative take-over within the complicated machinery of frontier conditions. The Officer Commanding 6th/13th Frontier Force, Lieutenant-Colonel D. Russell, was our efficient mentor on this occasion. Little did he or Taylor know that within a few short years Russell was destined to be our brigade commander in the Western Desert and, later, our divisional commander in Italy.

On a bitter winter day on the 20th of December, 1938, the

Battalion arrived in Razmak. On the following day they were engaged in road-protection duties in a blizzard, and for the remainder of the winter carried out normal duties, which included a prodigious amount of snow-clearing. The barracks were situated in the upper camp with a small but comfortable officers' mess, a highly prized lawn, English flower borders and a tennis court. Games were the order of the day. They kept the men fit and happy in a garrison which has been dubbed "the Empire's largest monastery." The inter-platoon and inter-company hockey tournaments for the cups presented by the grand old head clerk, Dost Mohamed, and Subadar-Major Ahmed Khan kept hockey enthusiasm and efficiency at a keen level. Each company could turn out two good teams, and the Battalion team, with John Auret, Lane, Subadar Sardar Khan and the perennial Havildar Gulistan as its leading lights (supported from the touchline by the vocal objurgations of the Commanding Officer and Taylor), kept its end up without setting Razmak on fire. At this time, also, soccer football was introduced, later to become a recreational stand-by on service.

During its two-year sojourn in Waziristan the Battalion formed part of the only three punitive columns which the Razmak Brigade sent out against the local tribesmen. It was not governmental policy during these turbulent years to "trail its coat" or to take official action against misdemeanours of other than intolerable defiance. This patient and wise policy, however irksome and unworthy it may have appeared to the military-minded, paid real dividends later when India was threatened with invasion from the east, and the notorious North-West Frontier Province remained unusually steady and friendly.

One of these columns deserves mention. In the spring of 1939 the Resident of Waziristan was shot at when passing Asad Khel on the Tochi road and his driver seriously wounded. The usual penalties were imposed but rejected by the local tribesmen, who refused, among other demands, to destroy the two towers near the road from which the shots had been fired.

Razcol was called into action. Making a forced march, the column arrived at Dam Dil at 4 o'clock in the afternoon. The recalcitrant tribesmen of Asad Khel watched the preparations for the night perimeter with some complacency. The Brigade Commander, Dennys, had two unsuspected cards to play. During the night he surrounded the village with three battalions, sent in the sappers to blow up the towers at dawn, and was back again in camp at Dam Dil by noon of the following day—with the expenditure of about one rifle magazine and no casualties. The surprise and secrecy required for this brilliant little operation were ensured by direct personal contact between the Brigadier and his unit commanders through the medium of portable wireless-telephony sets, these being used for the first time in frontier fighting.

Our Battalion, under the command of Major J. R. James, acting for Harvey, on leave, was the rearguard for the return march to Razmak. The tribesmen, exasperated by being outwitted, made vigorous attempts to exact some measure of vengeance. With the exception of a few minor casualties, the column marched into Razmak unscathed.

It may have been the anti-climax of Munich in conjunction with the intensely isolated way of life of a frontier garrison which caused the outbreak of war on the 3rd of September, 1939, to be accepted impassively, certainly philosophically, by the men. The subsequent "phoney war" in Europe seemed almost a picnic compared with the never-ending road-protection duties, lonely picquets, and the daily sniping of the local malcontent, "Bakshi Bill." The colourless B.B.C. reports and guarded newspaper comment gave little indication that within a short time this highly trained Indian garrison would be scattered to the four winds fighting against desperate odds from Singapore to Benghazi.

In September, 1940, the Battalion moved to Meerut to become mechanized for service overseas.

CHAPTER NINE

JULY, 1941—JUNE, 1942

MOBILIZATION

THE fall of France in June, 1940, and Mussolini's subsequent declaration of war left Britain and the Commonwealth alone to fight victorious Germany and resurgent Italy, whose superbly equipped armies, fleets and air forces lay athwart the Empire's communications in the Middle East. Even her best friends thought Britain's position hopeless. The War Cabinet, under the direction of Mr. Winston Churchill, made the strategic decision to give battle in North Africa and, for this fateful purpose—despite the appalling threat of invasion—stripped the United Kingdom to the bone, and asked India, Australia and New Zealand to send their men and equipment to this hazardous battle area.

The response was immediate, but only negligible in quantity to oppose the grandiose forces arrayed by Mussolini in Abyssinia, Eritrea, Libya and the Mediterranean littoral. Under the inspired leadership of Wavell this formidable host was bluffed, outmanœuvred, outfought and thrashed on many a great occasion. Our 4th Battalion was in the thick of this early fighting, and reports came trickling back to India of the value of mechanization, the dexterity of the sepoys in handling and maintaining motor transport, of the necessity of "light scale" living and fighting, of slit trenches, of navigation by the stars like mariners, of tank fighting with "Molotov cocktails," and of many other tactical devices peculiar to modern desert warfare.

Our Battalion did not reach the Middle East until August, 1941, and did not return to India until 1946. The official histories of these campaigns have yet to be written; the meagre official despatches are merely factual; the strategic background remains blurred and at times incomprehensible for want of knowledge, still secreted in official archives. We are too close to events to appraise them impartially. To describe, therefore, "Queen Mary's Own" minute part in this vast theatre is to isolate the

Battalion like a small spot-lighted figure in a tumultuous company of other splendid characters, and to leave the rest of the play, its drama, its tension and at times its purpose, badly drawn, nebulous and perhaps distorted. This is inevitable. The loss of the Battalion War Diaries in the break-out from Mersa Matruh in 1942 has, however, been amply compensated for by the Battalion's own Short History of its desert and Sicilian operations, printed in Cairo in 1945.

In these four years the Battalion reached the climax of its capital campaigning tradition. With its hundred years' experience of being knocked about in all climates, in all sorts and conditions and theatres of war, under the leadership of all kinds of officers from brilliant to mediocre, the Battalion preserved and enhanced its historical reputation. It accepted any challenge, any difficulty and any disappointment with the same fortitude and cheerful spirit which have been its abiding characteristics.

* * *

On arrival in Meerut in September, 1940, Harvey's training problems were formidable. The expansion of the Indian Army from a small, select, picked corps of regular units of two hundred thousand fighting men to a volunteer continental army of two million under arms was in progress. Before leaving Razmak the Battalion had been "milked" of approximately a hundred officers, non-commissioned officers and men as its contribution to the formation of the 6th and 7th Battalions of the Baluch Regiment. In the winter of 1940-41 further "milkings" took place to form the nucleus of the 8th, 9th and 14th Battalions. The egregious term "milking" was a euphemism invented by Army Headquarters to describe "skimming the cream," as, in fact, these drafts were hand-picked officers, Viceroy's commissioned officers, non-commissioned officers and specialists. Their places were filled by emergency commissioned officers from training schools in England and India and by promotion within the Battalion, while the rank-and-file strength was maintained by recruits from the ever-growing Training Battalion in Karachi.

For the first few months in Meerut the Battalion camped beneath the walls of the old Mutiny cemetery, but was later transferred to new temporary lines. We joined the 18th Infantry Brigade, part of the 8th Indian Division, then under formation. Mechanization, under the direction of the newly appointed Mechanical Transport Officer, Lieutenant R. Darkin, a tea planter from the Nilgiris, started at once. The first drivers were trained on civilian buses of the ramshackle type that plied on the roads. Gradually Service vehicles, mostly Chevrolets, came into supply, and within eight months the Battalion was fully mechanized with a large reserve of drivers. Considering that the average sepoy had never driven anything more complicated than a two-bullock-power cart, it was a remarkable illustration of the Indian soldier's adaptability. The standard of vehicle maintenance, the most difficult and important aspect of mechanical transport training, was kept high, and the number of accidents comparatively low. The inhabitants of the Meerut district wisely gave a wide berth and a clear passage when they saw a "learner" convoy of military lorries come jerking down the roads. Road march discipline, formations, leaguering, and problems of time and space, symbolized by the expressions "VTM" and "MIH," engrossed officers' thoughts.

In January, 1941, Harvey handed over command to Lieutenant-Colonel J. R. James, his Second-in-Command. In May Major W. E. Maxwell returned from his appointment on the Viceroy's staff, and took over Second-in-Command from Major L. White. At about this period it was decided by Army Headquarters to alter the Pathan composition of the Baluch Regiment. The Pathan strength was one-quarter of the Battalion, of which quarter one-third was Yusufzais and two-thirds Khattaks. This was changed topsy-turvily to one-third Khattaks and two-thirds Yusufzais, thus causing a complete block in Khattak promotions and opening up quick advancement for comparatively junior Yusufzai non-commissioned officers. Owing to mobilization the scheme had to be implemented at once, and undoubtedly upset and dismayed the eager Khattaks. Thanks largely to the tact and firm handling of the situation by the company commander, Captain Michael Forster, "B" Company settled down to its new organization with a good spirit.

Owing to the urgency of training and the manifold problems arising from mobilization and re-equipment, the hot weather in Meerut was a strenuous time. James's health broke down, and after his admission to hospital A. C. Taylor, now a lieutenant-colonel commanding the 9th Battalion, returned to take over command. As Taylor commanded the Battalion for the next three years of war, a synopsis of his military career will be of interest:

February, 1915.—Joined London Rifle Brigade as rifleman.
April, 1915.—Proceeded to France.
November, 1915.—Commissioned in the field and posted to 11th Battalion The Middlesex Regiment.
April, 1916.—Wounded. Hohenzollern.
July, 1916.—Awarded Distinguished Service Order, with a special mention to the effect that he was the youngest officer to be so decorated.
August, 1916.—Mentioned in despatches.
November, 1917.—Wounded at Arras.
September, 1918.—Transferred to Indian Army.
June, 1919.—Posted to 1st/127th Baluch Regiment.

After a year with the 2nd/127th Baluch Light Infantry Taylor rejoined our Battalion and served with it continuously until 1940, taking part in most of the events described in the previous chapter. The writer is indebted to one of the officers who served with him throughout the Desert campaign for the following pen-picture: "It's hard to pay an adequate tribute to Ack Taylor as C.O. through those early years overseas. He was beloved by the men as few officers I have known. The *Jawans* knew him as *Baba* (grand-dad), and such he was to them. He detested any form of 'bull,' and had a great instinct for fundamentals, giving his company commanders and staff a free hand over routine matters and trivialities provided they kept him informed of what they were doing. He had the reputation of being a difficult person to put over a fast one on, and had the power to penetrate through any smoke-screen of excuses. Strict and fair, his officers found him particularly sympathetic over their troubles, and ready with sound advice based on his large experience of life in general and regimental soldiering in particular. His hold on the Battalion was based on his knowledge and experience of handling men *and* his imperturbable leadership in times of crisis."

The officers who accompanied the Battalion when it set sail in H.T. *Nevassa* from Bombay on the 31st of July, 1941, were:
Lieutenant-Colonel A. C. Taylor, D.S.O.: Commandant.
Major W. E. Maxwell, C.I.E.: Second-in-Command.
Captain J. F. Robinson: O.C. H.Q. Company.
Captain A. Hamid Khan: O.C. "A" Company (Punjabi Musulmans).
Captain J. M. Forster: O.C. "B" Company (Pathans).

Second-Lieutenant J. M. Vokes: O.C. "C" Company (Dogra Brahmans).
Second-Lieutenant H. Nicholls: O.C. "D" Company (Punjabi Musulmans).
Captain W. H. M. Lane: Adjutant.
Captain G. Van Loo: Quartermaster.
Second-Lieutenant I. Fleming: Carrier Officer.
Second-Lieutenant R. H. Brown: Signal Officer.
Second-Lieutenant N. F. Canteenwala: Company Officer.
Lieutenant D. N. Vora, I.M.S.: Medical Officer.

The Mechanical Transport Officer, Second-Lieutenant Bill Williams, accompanied the Battalion transport, some seventy-five vehicles, in a later ship.

Of these officers, Vokes, Nicholls, Van Loo, Fleming, Brown, Canteenwala and Williams were emergency commissioned officers who had joined the Battalion since war broke out. Despite their junior rank and comparative inexperience, they had quickly fitted into the heavy responsibilities which the war had thrown upon them.

The Viceroy's commissioned officers were:

Subadar-Major Ahmed Nur.	Jemadar Kirpa Ram.
Subadar Akbar Khan.	Jemadar Gul Mohd.
Subadar Nasib Khan.	Jemadar Gulistan.
Subadar Shahra Khan.	Jemadar Allah Ditta.
Subadar Gopi Chand.	Jemadar Jaffar Shah.
Subadar Sultan Khan.	Jemadar Inayatullah.
Jemadar Hassan Gul.	Jemadar Ismail.
Jemadar Rahmat Khan.	Jemadar Dharam Pal.
Jemadar Bostan Khan.	Jemadar Walayat Ram.
Jemadar Ram Nath.	Jemadar Mohd Khan.

Headquarters of the 18th Infantry Brigade (Brigadier Lochner), with the 1st/2nd Gurkha Rifles, had already sailed. The third battalion of the Brigade, the 2nd/3rd Gurkha Rifles, was following in another transport. The Divisional Commander, Major-General C. O. Harvey, had already left India by air. Although the greatest secrecy encompassed our departure and our destination was a mystery, rumour and intelligent guessing had picked on Iraq as our probable objective. Since April, when Raschid Ali and his "Golden Square" formation of Nazi dupes had usurped power in Baghdad, we in India had watched the magnificent defence of Habbaniya by a Royal Air Force training school and one British battalion, and had learnt with relief at the end of May that Raschid Ali had been defeated and had taken to flight. In June Hitler had declared war on Russia, and the Nazi drive to the Caucasus was a developing threat to the whole Middle East. The oilfields of Iraq and Iran were becoming the focus of world attention. German intervention in Iraq and Vichy French overt assistance to Nazi infiltration and passage through Syria, threatened not only the pipe-lines but the oilfields themselves. So certain were officers that Iraq was our goal that they studied Arabic textbooks on board under the tuition of the Quartermaster, Van Loo, who had been an official in the Anglo-Iranian Oil Company. The voyage was hot with a rough sea, but uneventful.

PERSIA, 1941

As the *Nevassa* steamed up the Shatt-el-Arab on the 9th of August the Brigade Commander, Lochner, clambered aboard from a launch, and was closeted with the Commanding Officer and Second-in-Command for an hour. His information was as startling as it was agreeable. It was to the effect that on arrival in Basra the Battalion was to be split into three detachments for "hush-hush" operations. As secrecy was of supreme importance, no details of their role or location could be vouchsafed. Accordingly, on disembarkation that evening preparations were made for the dispersal of the Battalion to its various commitments. One detachment of two companies was to go to sea at once under the ægis of the Royal Navy and await sealed orders. Another company was to join another naval expedition. The fourth rifle company was to join the Royal Air Force for an undisclosed air-transported operation. As was to be expected, these mysterious projects created the liveliest satisfaction among all ranks, except the unfortunate personnel of Battalion Headquarters and H.Q. Company, to whom no role had been assigned.

BANDAR SHAHPUR

The first detachment, consisting of the two Punjabi Mussulman companies, "A" and "D," under the command of Major W. E. Maxwell, with one month's rations, two live sheep, tentage, cumbersome iron water tanks, and five hundred pounds in filthy

Persian paper currency packed in sandbags, embarked on the evening of the 10th of August in H.M.I.S. *Lawrence,* and slipped down the Shatt-el-Arab that night in great secrecy. The laconic sealed orders proved to be an anti-climax; under command of the Royal Navy (called Force "B"), the detachment was to assist in the capture of Axis merchant shipping anchored since the outbreak of war in the harbour of Bandar Shahpur, and to seize and hold Bandar Shahpur. Unfortunately, nobody on board (including the Navy) had ever heard of Bandar Shahpur, and no maps were supplied.

The next day the detachment transhipped in mid-ocean to H.M.A.S. *Kanimbla,* an Australian converted cruiser, the flagship of Force "B" (Captain W. Adams, R.N.). As the two ration sheep were pushed across the heaving single-plank gangway they were saluted punctiliously by the Australian sailors, who thought, reasonably enough, that they were our regimental mascots. The *Kanimbla* was a beautiful, commodious passenger liner, converted as a cruiser with an armament of 6-inch and 4-inch guns. The detachment lived on board—their quarters the spacious promenade decks—for over a fortnight, and were overwhelmed by the care and kindliness shown to them by the whole ship's company, from the Captain down to the latest-joined ordinary seaman.

During this warm fortnight strenuous training was carried out in handling Fleming boats and scaling vertical ladders with full equipment. The flotilla for the capture of the Axis shipping was gradually assembled at the hidden rendezvous in the Persian Gulf. It was a heterogeneous collection: H.M.I.S. *Lawrence,* H.M.Ss. *Cockchafer* and *Snapdragon* (the latter from the China Station), the tug *St. Athan* (straight from the Tobruk run), the tug *Arthur Kavanagh,* and even an Arabian dhow with an auxiliary engine. The Australian sailors referred to the force as "the Afghan Navy." Air photographs were received which gave details of the enemy moored in the deep-water harbour of Bandar Shahpur. There were eight ships altogether, four modern German ships of the Fels Line, the *Weisenfels, Hohenfels, Sturmfels* and *Marienfels,* and four Italian ships, the *Caboto, Bronte, Barbara* and another. These vessels were manned by skeleton crews totalling about sixty Germans and a hundred and twenty Italians. In addition, there was one, possibly two, Iranian gunboats and a six-thousand-ton Italian floating dock.

The Baluch detachment supplied one boarding party to augment the naval parties detailed to capture these ships. This consisted of Second-Lieutenant R. H. Brown, four lance-naiks and four sepoys. Their task in conjunction with some naval personnel was the boarding of the *Hohenfels*, believed to be the Axis flagship. They threw themselves into their specialized pirate training with enthusiasm, grew beards and assumed a gait and language more nautical than their instructors'.

Information regarding Bandar Shahpur was meagre until an oil-company tug master joined the expedition with first-hand information of the port and its lay-out. The town was the southern terminus of the Trans-Iranian railway, built on a reclaimed mud-flat ten miles south of the mainland proper, and approached only by the railway embankment. The last reputed military landing in this area was by Nearchus, Alexander the Great's admiral, on the return from India of the Macedonian invasion in 325 B.C. The tide rose eighteen feet, making it impracticable to land anywhere on the precipitous and greasy sea wall except at the single jetty. There was a garrison of a couple of platoons of Iranian infantry and no constructed defence works. This information solved many problems and simplified the operation orders for the landing. Maxwell constructed a model of the port on the floor of the orderly room, and every section commander was rehearsed in his exact role for the assault.

In the early hours of the morning of the 25th of August, 1941, the Russians moved upon Persia from the north, Major-General W. J. Slim's 6th Division from Iraq and Major-General C. O. Harvey's 8th Division from the south. During the night little Force "B" crept up the Khor Musa towards its objectives. Just before dawn the boarding parties grappled the Axis ships with their bamboo ladders. The German and Italian sailors, who were on the alert, opened their sea cocks and set fire to the barrels of petrol stacked around their bridges and officers' quarters amidships. The sky was illuminated with the flames of eight ships burning furiously. Methodically the Navy set about extinguishing the burning ships, the *Kanimbla* herself running alongside the largest vessel, the *Bronte*, and fighting the fire with all available men. By dawn the White Ensign was flying from every masthead. Only one ship, the *Weisenfels*, succeeded in scuttling herself successfully. She sank in the harbour, a burnt-out hulk, two days later. The remainder, fifty thousand tons of Axis shipping, two of them discovered later to be submarine supply ships, were being made seaworthy again in Indian harbours within a month. Brown's boarding party had a spirited action in the *Hohenfels,* whose crew resisted with jack-knives and grenades. Two Germans were killed before surrender was made, and the ship was taken intact.

Naval preoccupation with this holocaust delayed the landing operation and caused a last-minute change of the plan. As the Fleming boats had been immobilized by the fire-fighting activities, and the *Kanimbla* could not go alongside the jetty, which was occupied by two neutral cargo steamers, Captain Adams placed a captured harbour tug and the Arabian dhow at Maxwell's disposal. "A" Company (Captain Hamid Khan) and Detachment Headquarters embarked in these craft and set sail for the jetty, a mile distant. The landing, on a rickety ladder in single file on the jetty, was unopposed. Maxwell was met by a Persian rear-admiral, who surrendered his sword and the port. Hamid Khan and his company swept forward according to the original plan to take the railway station. After a brisk little encounter with two platoons of the 18th Iranian Infantry in the station yard, he put them to flight across the desolate marshes towards the north. Two Persian soldiers were killed. We had one sepoy wounded. By 0730 hrs. Bandar Shahpur was in our hands. "D" Company (Second-Lieutenant H. Nicholls) disembarked shortly afterwards, and mopping-up and organization of the port and railway were continued throughout the day. This reorganization holds a small story of some importance. At first the Persian rail and port officials refused to render any assistance to Maxwell, who was the local appointed representative of His Majesty's Government. Threats and bribes proved ineffective, and the situation appeared to have reached a deadlock, when a young Persian customs official asked Maxwell in English if the detachment was the same Baluch Regiment which had occupied Bushire in 1918. On being assured that it was the identical battalion this officer turned to his sullen compatriots and harangued them excitedly. The upshot was that they all then agreed to carry out their normal duties. Later he explained to Maxwell that his father had been a senior official in Bushire in 1918, and he had heard him speak of the good behaviour of the 127th Baluchis, a regiment from India.

That evening reports came in that a neighbouring oil-storage installation at Bandar Mashoor, with a high percentage of British officials among its employees, was in danger of being looted by marauding tribesmen. After a reconnaissance in a Persian gunboat, Maxwell sent "D" Company to defend it. The company was received with open arms and a fleet of useful trucks. Preparations were then made to "show the flag" in motor transport over a wide area of this southern province of Khuzistan, when—to the dismay of all—the "Cease Fire" was sounded by the B.B.C. on the night of the 28th of August.

HAFT KHEL

On the 10th of August Captain M. Forster and "B" Company moved to Shaibah airfield north of Basra. They spent the next fortnight in practising the techniques required for air-transported operations, then in their infancy. Six Vickers Valentia aircraft of good vintage years were allotted for the task, which was still a secret. On the 21st of August full orders for the operation were issued: "B" Company was to be landed in the oil station of Haft Khel in Iran, about a hundred and twenty miles north-east of Basra, from six troop carriers. On arrival the company was to collect the families of British and Indian personnel from the nearby station of Masjid-e-Suleman in transport to be supplied by the oil company, and bring them to Haft Khel, which was to be made a defended locality. The managers of Haft Khel and Masjid-e-Suleman were informed of the enterprise.

At 5 a.m. on the 25th of August "B" Company emplaned and flew off, escorted by Hurricanes. A "safe to land" signal was displayed on the small private landing ground at Haft Khel. The first flight of three machines made a perfect landing on inadequate and sloping ground. Two Valentias of the second flight were not so lucky, and crashed. Fortunately a Yusufzai platoon, who were the occupants, accepted this unceremonious first contact with Persian soil as part of the day's work, and scrambled out of the wreckage with only a few abrasions and minor cuts. Battle positions, as rehearsed in Shaibah, were taken up whilst the four remaining Valentias took off for their return journey within ten minutes. As they were waiting for the manager and the Masjid-e-Suleman transport to turn up, Forster and his headquarters encountered a group of Iranian police *sowars* on the airfield boundary. The police officer was ordered to hand over his revolver. He drew it, and deliberately fired five rounds at Forster's chest at five yards' range. Forster's orderly silenced him with a burst from his tommy-gun. Forster, miraculously unhurt, picked up the revolver and found five misfires in the chamber. His assailant was the local chief of police, and found to be an opium addict. Forster was to live and fight with the Battalion for the rest of the war, one of its staunchest veterans.

The company then proceeded to surround and disarm the local police station successfully. The manager of the oil installation declared that there was no transport available for the evacuation of the Masjid-e-Suleman families, but that his colleagues there were satisfied regarding their safety. It was a foolish lack of co-operation, as Masjid-e-Suleman was occupied the following day by the Iranian Army, but one which Forster was impotent to rectify. He put Haft Khel into a state of defence, and took small patrols in lorries to survey the surrounding villages and countryside. These quick-moving patrols were soon magnified into a useful rumour that Haft Khel was occupied by at least a battalion. Air reconnaissance reported that there was a large "OK" on the Masjid-e-Suleman's manager's roof, and when peace was declared on the 28th of August the situation was found to be quiet and satisfactory.

KURRAM SHAHR

The role of "C" Company (Second-Lieutenant J. M. Vokes) was a combined operation with the Royal Navy against the Iranian naval installation at Kurram Shahr. It proved to be a sterner ordeal than those faced by their comrades at Bandar Shahpur and Haft Khel. After a week's training in embarking and disembarking under all conditions "C" Company left Basra on the 24th of August in three small ships. Sailing down-stream, the force arrived at their position off Kurram Shahr at 3.55 a.m. on the 25th, and five minutes later the naval bombardment opened. One Iranian gunboat, tied up alongside, returned the fire, but was quickly silenced, and No. 13 Platoon boarded and captured the vessel.

The company was then landed to capture the shore installations, principally the naval barracks. The only opposition was encountered by No. 14 Platoon, whose objective was the enemy quarter-guard. In this action the company commander, Jimmy Vokes, whilst gallantly trying to cross a piece of ground under heavy fire to reach grenade-throwing distance, was mortally wounded. He continued to encourage his men, refusing any aid, until the objective was taken. His gallant conduct was commended by the Divisional Commander and the Chief Naval Officer. The Battalion could not easily spare this splendid young officer, who had been an inspiration to his Dogras by the wholehearted spirit with which he entered into all regimental activities. The company, on being relieved by the 1st/2nd Gurkha Rifles, returned the next day to Battalion Headquarters.

Thus ended the invasion of Persia. The oilfields and the overland route to Russia were safe. Some five hundred German technicians and "tourists" were rounded up before their plans for sabotage and Persian domination matured. Mr. Alan Moorehead, in "African Trilogy," sums up the operation in these words: "It was like no war I had ever seen before. . . . Months of planning had preceded this invasion. But the actual fighting, the actual event which changed the country's history, was really a very small thing. There was nothing here to be greatly excited about, nothing, apart from the technical smoothness of the operation, to be very proud of." We have seen in our Battalion's case how this technical efficiency was achieved. What was equally important was the almost gentle initiation into battle of a battalion, the bulk of which was young soldiers of under one year's service.

In the meantime Battalion Headquarters and H.Q. Company made a forlorn trek across the desert from Basra to Ahwaz, having collected the Mechanical Transport Officer, Williams, and the motor vehicles which had arrived from India. The Battalion was collected together again in a brigade camp at Kot Abdullah, a few miles south of Ahwaz, for further desert warfare training. It was here that the Brigade practised the technique of day and night movement in desert formations, and subsequently, by its experiments in this subject, contributed to the official training pamphlet on these complicated tactics.

At about this time Maxwell was recalled to India to command the newly raised 15th Baluch Battalion, and with him went Second-Lieutenant I. Fleming. Captain Robinson was appointed Second-in-Command, and Brown became Carrier Officer.

IRAQ AND PALESTINE, 1941

For the next three months the Battalion's wanderings in the wilderness show a haphazard pattern symptomatic of all alarums and excursions which were then the only common feature of the Middle East theatre. From Ahwaz in Persia to Tobruk in Cyrenaica is a considerable journey even as the crows fly. When complicated by uncertain stops at Baghdad, Mosul, Haifa and Suez, and frequent changes of transport, the expedition becomes an unforgettable experience and one which will test the resilience of a battalion in no small degree.

At the end of September, 1941, the Battalion and the 1st/1st Punjab Regiment were selected from the 8th Division as reinforcements for the Desert campaign. The first stop was Baghdad, reached by road and rail, where a halt was made for twelve days. We arrived in this unromantic capital a few hours after both the 1st and 4th Baluch Battalions had departed for unknown destinations. The next halt was at Mosul, where another month was spent awaiting the 2nd/5th Essex, whom we were relieving in the desert. We were employed in the interlude in helping to construct the oilfield defences.

The original plan to reach Palestine was via the Baghdad railway, through South Turkey and Syria, but, owing to objections by the Turkish Government this interesting journey was cancelled. Accordingly, the Battalion returned to Baghdad by rail, and was transported by a General Purposes Company of the Royal Indian Army Service Corps from Baghdad to Haifa, nearly six hundred miles across the Syrian Desert. This part of the journey took six days, from the 24th to the 29th of November, pleasant travelling in the cool winter sunshine, and made memorable by the hospitality given us by the oil company officials at the various pumping stations, where the night halts were made. Halfway across the desert some of the trucks developed serious engine troubles. Like a *deus ex machina*, there appeared an Australian workshop company, who threw themselves with delight into the necessary repairs. The convoy was fit and complete for the road the next morning. The last stage of this trip, a hundred and ten miles from Mafraq to Haifa, was through the green lands of the Jordan Valley and over the verdant slopes of Galilee. The Battalion had its evening meal in an olive grove at the foot of Mount Carmel, and the same night entrained for Egypt.

At Suez the happy interlude ended. There, stores, equipment and such transport as was deemed desert-worthy were taken over from the rear party of the 2nd/5th Essex. We had left in Mosul our complete fleet of almost new vehicles and, in their place, received six of the most dilapidated 15-cwt. trucks ever encountered since the original "Bazaar" buses issued for training in Meerut. The Battalion then went by rail to Mersa Matruh to join the Welch Regiment and the 1st/1st Punjabis in the 38th Indian Infantry Brigade. The motor transport was ordered to follow as best it could by road. Two days afterwards the Mechanical Transport Officer, Captain Williams, appeared with the transport—three trucks towing the remaining three. Instead of being welcomed with the respect and admiration deserved for such a remarkable feat of endurance, the sorry cortège was greeted with roars of laughter. Despite this derision, the lack of efficient transport was heart-breaking for a battalion which prided itself on its mechanization, and was to be a severe handicap for some months to come.

THE DESERT: I

During December, 1941, our new Brigade was engaged on line of communication duties between Mersa Matruh and an insignificant wayside railway station with the name of El Alamein. On the 24th of December the Battalion was ordered to Tobruk. It spent Christmas Day, 1941, in cattle trucks trundling through a raging sandstorm to railhead, Capuzzo. From various vehicle parks there an ill-assorted collection of trucks was mustered, and in these the Battalion arrived in Tobruk on the 1st of January, 1942.

To make the narrative clearer a brief synopsis of the Desert campaign is necessary. At the beginning of 1941 the forces of the Commonwealth had captured Benghazi. During the spring, however, the Axis Powers had struck with vigour and driven our forces back to the Egyptian frontiers. The summer was a stalemate, with both Auchinleck and Rommel building up their resources for the winter fighting. Tobruk remained in British hands, a constant source of irritation and danger on the German flank. Although Greece and Crete had fallen, the East African War had ended in sweeping victory. Eritrea, Italian Somaliland and Abyssinia had been overrun by Imperial forces. Three-quarters of Africa now lay safely behind our troops.

In November, 1941, Operation "Crusader" was put into operation, with Tripoli as its goal. The pendulum of this ever-moving campaign swung westward once again. Auchinleck, though weakened in his thrust by the new demand from the Far East, caused by Japan's entry into the war on the 6th of December, kept up the pressure. Rommel had retreated to his firm base at El Agheila, leaving garrisons at Bardia, Halfaya and Sollum which were unable to emulate the steadfastness of the Tobruk garrison, and were quickly subdued. Our advanced forces stood around Agedabia, which was also the limit of Wavell's advance in the previous winter. During January, 1942, the rain fell in torrents, grounding the air, slowing up supplies, and making the necessary build-up of stores and ammunition for a further advance a slow and tedious business.

Only two brigades, later to be joined by a brigade of Valentine tanks, could be mustered at Agedabia in direct contact with the enemy. The 4th Indian Division was at Benghazi, and scattered over some hundreds of miles to the rear were the remaining South Africans, British, New Zealanders, Indians, Poles and Fighting French—about five weak divisions in all. Rommel, always an opportunist, hit back in January with his superior German armour. By the 21st of January Benghazi had fallen again, and the pendulum started to swing back towards the east. The British forces threw up a defensive line at Gazala, and in February had halted the German onslaught.

This was the position during our Battalion's three-month sojourn in Tobruk, about thirty miles to the rear of the Gazala Line. Tobruk was the most advanced port of supply and therefore of considerable importance. A tempting target for Rommel's swift enveloping tactics, its defence had to be vigilant and resolute. Our role was to man the northern harbour defences and at the same time to maintain a mobile column to intercept any enemy raids from the south-west approaches. The Battalion was employed on these duties until relieved by the 2nd South African Division on the 20th of March. On relief our 38th Brigade moved to Qassassin via El Adem and Capuzzo. Early in April the Battalion was ordered to join the 5th Indian Infantry Brigade of the 4th Indian Division at Kabrit.

To become a part of this Division was a high honour. World-famous for its magnificent fighting record at Sidi Barrani, Eritrea and Keren in the early days of the war, the Division had added to its laurels for its unbroken record of great victories in 1941-42. Only at Benghazi, where it had been placed in a completely untenable position, had it suffered a reverse. Even then its 7th Brigade, commanded by a former Baluch officer, Brigadier R. H. Briggs, had made history by its spectacular break-out from German encirclement. In the subsequent withdrawal to the Gazala Line the other two brigades had fought a gallant rearguard action.

At Kabrit the Battalion was met by its new Brigadier, Russell, an old friend of Razmak days, and a few days later was inspected by Major-General F. S. Tuker, who, on behalf of his Division, bade us welcome. Shortly afterwards he took Taylor with him by air to see the defences of Cyprus, so it was guessed that some new job was pending. Orders then came for the Division to disperse: the 5th (our) Brigade to Palestine, the 7th to Cyprus, and the 11th to the Canal zone. By the 29th of April the Battalion was back again in Palestine. The camp was at Karkur, situated in the midst of flourishing farmlands with an abundance of water and green shade, providing a startling change from the arid conditions of the desert.

PALESTINE, 1942

The main task at Karkur was the protection of Haifa. This port was being put into a state of active defence against any possible Axis move on the oil refineries and pipe-lines. On the 18th of May His Royal Highness The Duke of Gloucester inspected the Battalion; a good parade, at which His Royal Highness expressed his pleasure at the bearing and turn-out of the men. At about this time also—although we did not know it—the Higher Command had heard that Rommel intended to resume his offensive on the 27th of May, the secret being divulged by a senior German officer in his cups in a Balkan capital.

In the race against time in the desert Rommel beat Auchinleck by a short head. The British ten-thousand-mile supply route round the Cape, compared with Rommel's quick channel crossing from Italy to Benghazi, was probably the deciding factor. The British had constructed a series of defensive localities, called boxes, from Gazala on the coast to Bir Hakim, some fifty miles due south on the open flank of the desert. The opposing armies were roughly equal with approximately a hundred and thirty thousand men and four to five hundred tanks, and their guns and air forces were fairly evenly matched in quantity. Only a trickle of heavy American armour had made its appearance. The main boxes were at Gazala, at a point a few miles south called Knightsbridge, at Bir Hakim and El Adem, while Tobruk itself, as we know, was a specially large box.

Rommel attacked on the 26th of May by an outflanking movement round Bir Hakim. For the next nineteen days the battle ebbed and flowed, with the German panzer divisions milling around and through the defensive localities, giving and taking awful punishment. By this time, after three weeks' combat, it would appear that the Higher Commands on both sides had lost grip or control of the main battle—with groups of panzers roving about no longer operating under sustained direction, and the British boxes proving to be traps when communications broke down.

THE DESERT: II

On the 3rd of June the 5th Indian Brigade was ordered to be ready to return to the Western Desert at one hour's notice. On the 8th of June the advance party of the Regiment left by road, the remainder entraining the same evening for Amariya, a station twenty miles west of Alexandria: thence by uneasy stages to railhead, now El Mushiffa. There, on the 13th of June, Taylor met Major-General Briggs, now promoted to command the 5th Indian Division. He told him of the fate that had befallen our old comrades of the 4th/10th Baluchis in the Knightsbridge Cauldron. Only five officers and a hundred and ninety men escaped. Taylor promised to supply a draft when required to bring them up to strength again. (Subsequently, owing to our own casualties, this promise could not be fulfilled.)

From all sides reports came in that the situation was critical. Into this vortex the Battalion plunged. Six anti-tank guns were handed out to each battalion in the Brigade, and a few hours given to train the sepoy gunners. The complement of eleven carriers was increased to twenty-one, with the adaptable sepoy given one day to learn his duties as crew. The confusion of the battle became apparent in the next few days. On the 15th/16th of June the Brigade moved to a box called "The Kennels." Whilst preparing this position it was relieved by elements of the 1st South African Division on its way back from Gazala, and ordered to another box, called "The Playgrounds." On arrival

Brigadier Russell was giving out his orders for the occupation of the Playgrounds when he was interrupted by his Brigade Major: "Excuse me, sir, but there's a chap here who says we have to move to Sollum tomorrow." And so it was. On the 19th of June the Brigade was ordered to leave the 5th Indian Division and join the 10th Indian Division, which was engaged in preparing the Sollum Line, some sixty miles to the rear of the battlefront. The organization of these rapid moves, the necessary reconnaissance, and the physical toil involved—quite distinct from the appalling fog of war enshrouding everything—can better be imagined than described.

On reaching Sollum an incident occurred which relieved some of the strain. The Battalion had to take over a sector of the line from a regiment of the French Foreign Legion. The legionaries refused to hand over, as they said a battle was imminent, and our Battalion had to spend the night behind the French position. In the morning the argument was resumed with some vigour on both sides, resulting in an unofficial compromise by which both units shared the sector. On the intervention of higher authority the French were persuaded to leave in the afternoon. During the night they crept back and occupied our old position in the rear in a "trigger-happy" frame of mind. Fortunately the night passed peacefully.

The 21st and 22nd of June were busy days in preparing the defences on a tenuous line of some two thousand five hundred yards, with a "tactical gap" on our left of two thousand yards, separating us from the 1st/4th Essex. The anti-tank weapons allotted to this sector were our own six 2-pounder guns and one troop of Royal Artillery under command; a flea against an elephant. On the 22nd of June the dire news came that Tobruk had fallen, with its great loss of men and material. Egypt, it seemed, now lay wide open before Rommel's armour. Stragglers from Tobruk and the forward areas came pouring through with reports that numerous enemy columns were advancing fast. Their advanced guards could be expected within an hour or two. The Battalion stood-to all day, but that evening the Brigade was ordered to evacuate the Sollum Line and retire to Matruh.

The Brigade moved during the night, the rearguard (the great 4th/6th Rajputana Rifles) having to extricate itself by fighting the forward elements of the fast-approaching enemy. The Brigade spent the next night in leaguer near Talata, and the following night at Fuka, before reaching Matruh on the 25th of June. These continual rearward moves were incomprehensible to the Indian soldier, who was at a loss to understand why we did not stand and fight. The Sollum Line had been only a screen to protect the invaluable transport of the Eighth Army which for the past few days was streaming eastward and down the Sollum Pass.

MERSA MATRUH

"On June 24 the 10th Division," writes the official historian in *The Tiger Kills,* "was able to report in at Mersa Matruh at more or less full strength, having moved 125 miles across a waterless plain in forty-eight hours, shadowed, harassed and ground strafed constantly by an enemy who had now exceeded his previous bound of advance, and who felt himself to be on the road to victory. . . . On June 25 armoured car patrols reported sixty-five enemy tanks accompanied by 2,000 motor transport to be approaching Mersa Matruh. That morning an Indian brigade occupied the western sea coast sector of Matruh perimeter, with another on the left, holding the airfield and the escarpment as far as Charing Cross. The 5th Indian Brigade (including our Battalion) then took up the line, and facing to the south and south-west, covered the arid desert approaches from the direction of Qaryet Riguh. Beyond the 5th Indian Division, which now consisted of the 9th and 29th Brigades, both very weak, held Sidi Hamza, 20 miles to the south of Mersa Matruh. Here the crescent of British minefields ended. . . .

"On June 26 the enemy was bearing down on Charing Cross, seven miles south of Matruh, on top of the escarpment with 100 tanks and 3,000 motor transport. The Sabratta and Trentino Italian Divisions were identified as closing up behind the German spearhead. Far to the south another armoured force was by-passing Matruh. A last train left on June 25 with heavy equipment, and it was realized that within a matter of hours the garrison would be isolated. On the afternoon of 25th June the last of the British armoured forces dropped back through the Mersa Matruh minefield and the gaps were mined."

That sets the stage. Our Battalion's part in the subsequent operation will bear close scrutiny. Before taking up its position on the southern sector, a complete rifle company with some non-essential transport, under the command of the Second-in-Command, Major Robinson, was ordered to be sent to the rear as "left out of battle" troops. "D" Company was selected for this disappointing role, as it was felt that its comrades in "A" Company would maintain the Punjabi Musulman standard in battle. "D" Company went back to Amariya, about twenty miles west of Alexandria.

On the 27th of June the Battalion moved south in battle formation: "A" Company (Captain H. Khan) on the right, "B" Company (Captain J. M. Forster) on the left, Battalion Headquarters in rear and centre of forward companies, and "C" Company (Captain Chatterji) in rear, followed by "B" Echelon of the Battalion transport. The Carrier Platoon brought up the rear as rearguard. The intention was to move south for four miles, then to move eastward to cover a gap in the minefields which might be used by the enemy to cut off the Matruh garrison. The Battalion had moved about four miles when it found the battalion ahead, the 1st/4th Essex, pinned to the ground by intensive enemy shell fire. No advance in that quarter was possible. Taylor sent "C" Company to work its way round the east flank of the Essex to a ridge about a mile distant. This move succeeded, and the Battalion then joined "C" Company on its ridge, accompanied by the battery under command. Intensive fire stopped further progress. Enemy concentrations and tanks could plainly be seen on another ridge about one thousand six hundred yards to the front. They appeared to be moving eastwards.

That afternoon another attempt was made to get on to the objective, but owing to the intensity of artillery and mortar fire no advance was possible. It was decided to leaguer *in situ* for the night. In the meantime our intelligence had discovered that the 50th (Northumbrian) Division had worked its way round to our front, and that it was, in fact, elements of this famous formation which could be seen moving about on our objective! Orders were received for the Battalion to move forward at 2200 hrs. and make contact. Sceptical as Taylor must have felt regarding the accuracy of this information, so confused and tangled were all movements and so opaque the fog of war that he had no option but to go forward and confirm the rumour.

Instead of meeting the 50th Division, the Battalion was hailed with the concentrated fire of every calibre of enemy weapon. The Battalion got a footing on the ridge, but was eventually forced off. In this wicked little assault Second-Lieutenant Frey, Officer Commanding the Carrier Platoon, fifty other ranks, and twelve carriers were lost. They were employed as advance and flank guards, and of necessity bore the brunt of the fire brought down upon the Battalion. Twenty wounded men were safely evacuated to the original leaguering area, to which the Battalion returned, bloody but unbowed. Frey and several of his platoon, it was learnt later, were made prisoners.

The remainder of the night was spent in digging in—to resist the German dawn attack, which was confidently expected. Dawn broke, but no attack. Instead, salvo after salvo came over. Any enemy vehicles which approached our position for closer inspection received a warm welcome from the Mortar Platoon. At midday on the 28th of June fresh orders were received to send out a company to try once again to make contact with the elusive 50th Division. "A" Company, with three carriers and a Royal Artillery carrier as observation post, set out towards the enemy on this mission. The enemy, hoping perhaps to lure them well into their position, did not interfere with this sally. Fortunately for Hamid Khan and his Punjabi Musulmans a wireless message recalled them before the company had penetrated too far.

A grim development had arisen. Taylor had been summoned to Brigade Headquarters to hear the news that the enemy had broken through well to the east, had cut the coast road, and, bluntly, had completely surrounded the 10th Indian Division. From any military standpoint the position appeared to be pretty hopeless—except for the slender chance that the enemy's intelligence was as chaotic as ours in this swift-moving operation. If he were momentarily unaware of the rich plum within his grasp, or in his pride imagined that the Division was sealed off effectively enough and could be mopped up later, there was the sporting chance that a determined break-out that night might catch him off his guard. Orders were given for the three brigades to make the attempt.

Taylor was given a free hand to extricate the Battalion and its attached troops. The two major problems confronting him were the composition of the break-out force, and its direction. Should he disperse the Battalion into company groups and with them make separate radial attacks on the encircling forces, a method giving easier control at night and permitting perhaps some to escape in the great confusion? Or should he concentrate the Battalion, with its attached personnel of all arms, and make one combined bull-like rush at the Germans? Should he make for the well-known coast road, aiming for Fuka, and join the stream of the retreating Eighth Army? Or should he chart a new unknown southerly course and break back, when he had shaken off pursuit, eastward towards Egypt?

Taylor, in his wisdom, decided on the last of these alternatives: firstly, to break through as a battalion, and, secondly, to avoid the coast route and strike out on a southerly detour for El Alamein. The course was marked on the maps: along the 727 grid line on a bearing of 235 for two miles, then south for eleven miles, and east again on a bearing of 11 for El Alamein. Time: 2140 hrs. It was a moonlit night. All surplus kit—baggage, stores and documents—was destroyed. Speed: twenty to twenty-five miles per hour. Every man was ordered to fire at any hostile movement.

In *The Tiger Kills* there is this vivid description:

"*The Baluchis in particular had a nasty job. The way out was over the ridge they had captured the night before, only to be blown off it again. In fact the battalion had to charge straight through a position known to be strongly held by the enemy. The charge started. All along the immediate front flare after flare rose into the sky, which with the light of the moon made the desert as light as day. The ridge was reached in safety, but then hell was let loose. Many enemy batteries were trained on the battalion and salvo after salvo short range ploughed through the charging trucks. Machine-gun bullets tore through the battalion and soon the area was blotted out in dust and smoke, lit by the red glare of burning lorries. But through the inferno the battalion rushed at a speed of about thirty miles an hour, swerving to avoid derelicts and slit trenches, bumping, jumping, swaying, with the fast revving engines roaring through the night.*

"*Then the leading trucks struck a newly laid minefield. The Baluchis slowed down and swerved away, which was just what the enemy anti-tank guns were awaiting. From every quarter, in front, both sides, and even behind they opened up. But although they appeared to be in the very jaws of hell, nothing could stop this battalion. With trucks and lorries burning furiously all around, the Baluchis charged on.*

"*The battalion carriers, in the meantime, had swerved the other way to deal with a line of anti-tank guns. Every single one of the carriers was destroyed in this very gallant effort, but not before Naik Mian Gul had rushed the nearest gun, killing all* the crew, then switched on to another and dealt with it in the same way before his carrier went up in flames. Only three men of the whole platoon survived, one of whom was Mian Gul, who jumped a passing truck.

"The battalion was now through the outer defences and came up against entrenched infantry. The sight of two hundred trucks and lorries roaring down on them was too much for the infantry soldiers. They clambered from their trenches and fled from the path of the onrushing vehicles. From every truck and every lorry poured a hail of death as the Indian soldiers seized their chance to have a hit back at the enemy."

On emerging from this shambles the Battalion and its attendant troops found themselves scattered, broken into fragments, and off their chartered course. The main danger lay in the panzers, sent out to destroy them, which could be heard prowling around in all directions. Avoiding these clanking monsters, individual trucks and small groups of vehicles coalesced into larger bodies and, making their way eastward on flat springs and almost empty tanks, using the stars as guides, reached the El Alamein area during the morning of the 29th of June.

On being mustered the casualties suffered by our Battalion, both in the engagements on the 28th and in the break-out, were not as heavy as Taylor feared. They were:

Officers

Second-Lieutenant Frey	Missing
Jemadar Ismail Khan	Missing
Jemadar Ram Nath	Missing
Jemadar Jumna Das	Missing
Jemadar Zaristan	Wounded

Other Ranks

Killed	4
Wounded	12
Wounded and missing	1
Missing	112

It was estimated that twenty-four hours after the break-out sixty per cent. of the 10th Division had reached safety, fighting their way through the four German divisions which lay in their path.

The Battalion was delighted when Taylor was granted, as an immediate award, a bar to his Distinguished Service Order for his part in these operations. The citation reads:

"On the 27th June, 1942, in face of considerable opposition, Lt. Colonel A. C. Taylor, Comdg. 3 Baluch, gained a footing on the escarpment in Square 7232, south of Matruh, thus drawing enemy forces on to himself, for the benefit of others. The enemy reinforced his troops in this area, but, in spite of this, on the night of 28/29 June, Lt-Col. Taylor again forced his way up the escarpment with his Battalion; broke through the enemy lines and succeeded in extricating most of his column. Throughout this operation Lt-Col. Taylor showed considerable drive, resource, tactical skill, and coolness under fire."

The gallant Naik Mian Gul was also awarded an immediate Indian Distinguished Service Medal.

In the depressing conditions then prevailing around El Alamein there was certainly one unit whose morale and fighting spirit were undiminished by the disasters which had overtaken our desert armies. By valour and sheer determination the 3rd Baluch had won through against the most impossible odds, and the men were elated and rightly proud of themselves. Mersa Matruh will always hold an honourable place in the Battalion's history.

CHAPTER TEN

JUNE, 1942, TO AUGUST, 1943

EL ALAMEIN: JUNE TO NOVEMBER, 1942

THE scattered remnants of the 5th Indian Brigade came together again around El Alamein on the 30th of June and the following days. The Brigade, less the 1st/4th Essex, was then sent to Mena, twenty miles from Cairo, to refit. It arrived at this peaceful location at 1300 hrs. on the 4th of July, but at 1900 hrs. on the same day orders came for its immediate return to the front.

Earlier in this Middle East campaigning the Quartermaster of the Battalion, Captain Van Loo, came to notice as an instructor in Arabic. It is full time to pay tribute to him and his "Q" staff on whom an immense burden fell, and kept falling, with every changing location and attachment to different formations. The "Q" staff work in the Middle East, from the highest in command to the lowest unit, will probably be considered by future historians as a supreme example of military efficiency. Equipment, rations, clothing and, above all, water were a quartermaster's incessant nightmare. Throughout our changing fortunes Van Loo, energetic, keen and uninhibited by red tape, accepted his responsibilities with good humour and indefatigable pertinacity. Like other quartermasters in our history, he often had to dispense with the formalities of indents and "usual channels," and use the suasion of charm and *bonhomie* to procure the goods. The main point was—the goods were always delivered. Tireless in all his pursuits, this happy officer managed to achieve both courtship and marriage during his war-time service with the Battalion.

It will occasion no surprise, therefore, to learn that within three hours the Battalion was on the move again, this time to Bahig, thirty miles east of Alamein. Four days were spent in this assembly area collecting transport, weapons and equipment. A new draft to replace casualties arrived. On the 9th of July the Brigade moved forward to take over from the 9th Australian Brigade, who were in reserve in the area of Point 93, on the rear limb of Ruweisat Ridge.

El Alamein had long been appreciated as a superb tactical position for defence. In this desert war it was unique in that both its flanks were guarded: on the north by salt lakes and the sea, on the south by the Qattara Depression, a geological freak of broken cliffs and little plateaux, eroded by the centuries and untankable. The whole position was only forty miles in length from the Mediterranean to the Depression. In the centre was the Ruweisat Ridge, a hog's-back eminence rising imperceptibly from the desert in the west and running back parallel with the coast, ending abruptly in a high bluff well within the British zone. It was a long, minatory forefinger pointing straight into Rommel's stomach. Between this feature and the sea was the less dominating Alamein Ridge, running parallel. Although Rommel was on the threshold of Egypt (and Mussolini was preparing his uniforms for his state entry into Alexandria), Auchinleck, now Supreme Commander, had succeeded in extricating the Eighth Army, and was establishing it on this line of great natural strength. It is the destruction of the enemy forces in the field, and not the capture of place-names on a map, which brings victory. Rommel had not yet achieved this consummation of his ambition, and the exhaustion of his troops at the end of a long line of communication, despite their high spirit, was a source of weakness. During the next few months he made several desperate attempts to break the British line, and failed. He stabbed at the 9th Australian Division (the famous "Rats of Tobruk") on the Alamein Ridge, and was repulsed; he swung round to probe the New Zealanders' defence on the southern flank, and his spearhead was snapped off. He made fruitless efforts to drive or blast the Indian Division off the Ruweisat Ridge. With these stern trials of strength we are intimately concerned.

The 3rd Baluch came to grips early. On the 15th of July the 5th Brigade was sent forward to capture and hold Point 63 and Point 64 on the Ruweisat Ridge. On the right the 3rd Baluch, with Point 63 as the objective; on the left the 4th/6th Rajputana Rifles to take Point 64. Owing to enemy observation, no detailed reconnaissance was possible. To achieve the maximum of surprise a night attack was ordered at 2200 hrs. without any artillery support. The Battalion order of battle was as follows:

"C" Company (Captain Chatterji) on the right.
"D" Company (Lieutenant Sardar Ali) on the left.
Two platoons of "B" Company in support of "D."

"A" Company (Captain Hamid Khan) in reserve.
Battalion Headquarters in the centre and forward with "C."
The remainder of the Battalion to remain on the starting line until the objective was captured.

At midnight the leading battalions silently slipped through the wire covering the British minefield, and moved towards their objectives from the south-east. The enemy—Italians—were caught napping, and by dawn the Battalion was on its objective with a bag of forty prisoners. Unfortunately the Rajputana Rifles, in closer contact with the enemy, had encountered minefields, wire and heavy fire in the darkness, and were unable to move forward. On seeing this in the morning, Taylor sent "D" Company to get round the minefield. The company got a precarious footing on Point 64, but was forced back by heavy mortar fire. In this engagement Lieutenant Sardar Ali was wounded. Later during the morning the Rajrif penetrated the minefield and took their objective, overwhelming two battalions of the Brescia Division and capturing a thousand prisoners. New Zealanders came up on the left and the ground was consolidated. A happy signal from the Divisional Commander, General Briggs—"Well done, Baluchis!"—warmed all hearts.

This brilliant little success, which gained high ground for observation and gun positions to outflank any tank thrust between the two main ridges, provoked the inevitable counter-attack. On the morning of the 16th of July, after continuous shelling, a heavy armoured attack on the New Zealanders forced them back, thus isolating the 5th Brigade on its advanced promontory. The day had been spent in digging into the stony surface whenever a brief respite from shelling occurred. During the night these inadequate defences were feverishly strengthened.

An intercepted enemy message confirmed what had been suspected—the Germans were forming up for an armoured attack in the Deir el Shein Depression, to the north-west of our position. (This depression was, and still is, of melancholy interest to our Battalion. In it, a fortnight previously, our first war-time brigade, the 18th, which we had left at Ahwaz, now hurriedly called from Iraq to help to stem the German onrush into Egypt, had been sadly mauled by the triumphant panzers. On his way back from Matruh, the Adjutant, Lane, had met the newly arrived brigade and had been able to put them "in the picture." Shortly afterwards they were overrun.)

During the day strong reinforcements in the shape of a British armoured brigade with a strong force of the new long-barrelled 6-pounder anti-tank guns, arrived and took up a position in the lee of Point 64. Stuka attacks—the most menacing, if perhaps the least effective of all air tactics—had been intensified during the day, and it was fully realized that Rommel now intended to recapture the two points. The attack was launched in the evening, the sinking sun blinding the eyes of the defenders.

"Twelve hundred yards from the Brigade's position enemy tanks emerged over a low ridge. A hail of solid shot crashed into them. The infantry crouched in their sangars and slit trenches, while a furious battle raged overhead. As darkness fell streams of interlacing tracers crossed as the secondary armament of the rival tanks engaged. Light armour and armoured cars skirmished out to meet each other, and shortly deadly exchanges occurred. Towards midnight silence fell. Rommel's attack had got nowhere." (The Tiger Kills.)

With the morning light the extent of his failure was manifest. The battleground was strewn with scrap metal. Twenty-four smashed panzers, six armoured cars, ten anti-tank guns, eight 75-mm. field guns, and six of the legendary 88-mm. dual-purpose guns littered the area. Our casualties in the 3rd Baluch for the two days were light. They were:

Officers
- Lieutenant Sardar Ali .. .. Wounded
- Subedar Sultan Khan .. .. Wounded
- Jemadar Dharm Pal.. .. .. Wounded

Other Ranks
- Killed 4
- Wounded 16

The 5th Brigade remained master of Ruweisat Ridge, and was to remain there until the Battle of Alamein. It was a foul spot. The ridge itself was of rough stone with a few inches of fine dust which arose in dense clouds with every passing vehicle. The heat and the flies were an unceasing torment. Stuka dive-bombing and harassing artillery fire plastered the whole region every day. The valley between the two points was nicknamed "Death Alley," as it was the Stukas' favourite target. The only practical protection was camouflaged sangars and shallow slit trenches. Boredom was to some extent obviated by the forays and patrols carried out nightly to probe the enemy's positions, to identify units, and collect information for the plan which was being evolved for the coming battle. The Brigade was still under the command of the 5th Indian Division, which had organized the ridge as a divisional locality with a routine programme of rest and relief reminiscent of the war in France from 1914 to 1918.

One of the most ambitious of the patrols carried out in this sector was organized by Captain Forster and his Pathan company. The intention was to raid the Deir el Shein Depression, now a heavily defended locality, and bring back prisoners for identification. The eastern rim of the depression joined the ridge in a series of peninsulas, all wired and protected by minefields. One of these peninsulas was selected as the objective.

The raid was mounted on a truly elaborate scale. Three regiments of artillery were in support. Careful binocular reconnaissances were made as close up as possible, air photographs were studied, and on the day before, General Briggs came and discussed the project with "B" Company. The platoons were commanded by senior non-commissioned officers. On the night of the 12th of August the company set forth on its preliminary advance to the forming-up place (F.U.P.), a stealthy compass march of one thousand two hundred yards due north and then two thousand yards due west. The plan was for No. 12 Platoon to make a breach in the enemy wire and defend the gap; for No. 11 Platoon to go through this breach and form a bridgehead of about two hundred yards in depth. No. 10 Platoon was to carry out the actual raid and collect the prisoners—an operation estimated to take five minutes.

At midnight the supporting artillery put down a shattering barrage. Under this cover the company, with No. 12 Platoon in the lead, doubled forward. It was in this last advance that the plan miscarried. Instead of hitting the tip of the peninsula, they advanced over some six hundred yards of ground before running into the enemy wire in a re-entrant between two peninsulas. Cutting their way rapidly through this, the operation continued according to plan, No. 11 Platoon rushing through and fanning out, firing from the hip. Then, for the first time, enemy small-arms fire opened up from both flanks, enfilading the wire, but did not stop No. 10 Platoon and company headquarters getting through. They advanced over several enemy trenches and emplacements—all empty. More strong wire covered by automatic fire halted them. By this time, the enemy, now thoroughly aroused, was bringing down fire from machine guns and mortars from all directions. The smoke, noise and dust in the darkness broke up communications between the platoons. Forster fired a green Very light as the signal for withdrawal. His company was virtually enclosed in a box of automatic fire, but he managed to extricate No. 10 Platoon and its severely wounded commander, Havildar Gul Badshah, and a few stragglers of No. 12 Platoon. Touch was lost with No. 11 Platoon, but the remainder of the company succeeded in reaching the F.U.P. by timing their rushes through the gaps of machine-gun tracer fire. Forster reported back to Battalion Headquarters at 0200 hrs., and No. 11 Platoon (who had not seen the Very signal) rejoined an hour later. Its commander, Havildar Sher Aslam, had made his own appreciation of the situation and, although pinned to the ground for some time, had managed to dribble his men in pairs through the gap. For his leadership on this occasion he was later mentioned in despatches. The casualties suffered in this raid were five wounded and six missing.

As a matter of interest it might be observed that similar raids carried out by the divisions on either flank were also abortive. No one ever broke the defences of Deir el Shein, and after the Battle of Alamein it was discovered that the enemy defences in this sector were among the most elaborately engineered on the whole Alamein front.

On the 9th of September the 5th Indian Division was relieved at Ruweisat by the 4th Indian Division. This made no change in our fortunes, as the 5th Brigade merely reverted to its original formation, and stayed on the ridge. Our only relief was an occasional spell in an area called "Position 'C'," a defended locality ten miles east on the ridge. During one of these spells the Brigade was loaned to the 44th (Home Counties) Division and spent three weeks in what was called "The New Zealand Box." Taylor, who had been acting as Brigade Commander, returned at this time from his Brigade duties. The Battalion was now wearing the 4th Indian Division "Red Eagle" flash. This famous insignia was the gift of the women of the Punjab, suggested by its Prime Minister, the late Sir Sikander Hayat Khan, and was to become one of the most coveted emblems of the whole Eighth Army.

The Battle of Alamein began at 2130 hrs. on Friday, the 23rd of October, 1942. The role of the 4th Division in the opening phases of the battle was to contain the enemy in the centre, gripping him tight, pinning him to his ground and preventing any movement to his threatened flanks. The 5th Brigade was called upon to form the Corps reserve for the XXX Corps. Moving forward gradually through the next few nights, the Brigade found itself by the 28th of October in an area some miles north-west of its summer quarters, in the low ground between the two main ridges. Shelling was slight, but the area was infested with booby-traps and any move off the beaten tracks had fatal results.

On the 3rd of November the Brigade received orders to attack a feature called Kidney Ridge. This was probably the climacteric of this momentous battle, the moment which General Montgomery selected to drive paths into the enemy's centre for the British armour to pour through and administer the *coup de grâce*.

Of necessity the plans for the Brigade attack had to be hurried. The Brigadier and his battalion commanders finished their reconnaissance at 1500 hrs. The attack was ordered for that night at one minute to midnight. As the company commanders were making their reconnaissances an intensive barrage was put down over the area, causing delay and more waste of precious time. The battalions were back some eight miles from the start line, and under their adjutants started to move forward in trucks in the fast-failing light of a winter evening. The going was appalling: patches of loose sand, the dust of thousands of moving vehicles, and the Stukas diving overhead. When darkness fell—there was no moon—conditions worsened and vehicles became bogged. The company commanders went back to find their trucks embedded in the sand, four miles from the start line, and with visibility about four feet. Zero hour was approaching, and it looked as if the attack could not be made that night. Russell had to change his original plan, and by fine staff work managed to have the artillery barrage postponed until a later hour. Our original place on the right of the attack was given to two companies of the Rajrif, with the Essex on the left and the 3rd Baluch in reserve. The men abandoned their trucks and marched forward, the carriers towing the vehicles carrying the support weapons. It was a desperate night of improvisation and hurried reorganization.

At 0230 hrs. the attack was launched with a concentration of four hundred guns on a front of eight hundred yards. This barrage marched across the minefields at the rate of a hundred yards in three minutes. The Brigade leant right up against it, and advanced steadily, meeting little opposition. Any enemy survivors were quickly dealt with. On through the night marched this devastating phalanx, halting at precise intervals to re-form and mop up. When the infantry got beyond the range of the field guns the medium and heavy guns took up the chorus without pause or falter. As first light came the barrage lifted, and there was silence. A short, sharp fight with the remnants of the enemy, and Kidney Ridge was in our hands. The Brigade had gone clean through the enemy lines for a distance of five miles. The climax came as rank after rank of British tanks came roaring through the gap, and swung north for the kill. The Battle of Alamein was over.

The next day the Battalion was ordered south to the Qattara Depression (with one battery of the Royal Artillery and one squadron of South African armoured cars under command) to round up pockets of enemy left behind. Then back for a week to the Shein Depression to engage in salvage operations, and see by daylight the scene of "B" Company's raid. The honour of pursuing Rommel's broken forces across Cyrenaica had been given to the Highlanders and the New Zealanders, with two armoured divisions. The task assigned to the 4th Indian Division of picking up scrap on the Alamein battlefield was only a temporary misfortune.

AFTER ALAMEIN

On the 15th of November, 1942, the Battalion moved to the coast at El Imayid for a period of rest, which the reader will agree was almost overdue. Individual training was begun, and as many men as possible were sent on short leave to the Delta. Within three weeks, however, the 5th Brigade was on the move again, this time to its old haunts of Tobruk, where it arrived on the 9th of December. At about this time Brigadier Russell was promoted to command the 8th Indian Division, and Taylor once again took over the Brigade, leaving Robinson in command of the 3rd Baluch. On the 3rd of January, 1943, the Brigade was ordered to Agedabia and, to practise desert formations, the overland desert route was selected for the move. Heavy seasonal rain turned the sand into mud, and after six days' floundering the Brigade was glad enough to be diverted into Benghazi on the 10th of January. In the meantime, General Montgomery had called for an Indian guard for his Eighth Army Headquarters. Two platoons of "A" Company (Punjabi Musulmans) under Lieutenant R. H. Brown were detailed for this interesting task. Subsequently they were the first Indian troops to march into Tripoli with General Montgomery's famous caravan.

At Benghazi the Brigade was laboriously employed in unloading ships and supplying working parties for harbour installations. Nevertheless, time was found to put three companies through the Benghazi Street Fighting School course, learning the technique required, it was hoped, for the fighting which lay ahead in Tripoli and Tunisia. Brigadier D. Bateman (another Baluch) arrived to take over the Brigade, and Taylor resumed command of the Battalion. On the 8th of February, 1943, came a sad blow. Orders were received to return to the Delta to relieve the 1st/9th Gurkhas as the divisional reserve battalion. The Divisional Commander, Major-General F. S. Tuker, personally asked Taylor to see that all ranks still wore the Red Eagle, and published the following farewell message in Divisional Orders:

"The Divisional Commander and all ranks of the 4th Indian Division part with 3/10 Baluch Regiment with the deepest regret. They leave in order to give one of the Division's affiliated units a chance to see active service.

"The 4th Division will never forget the gallantry and the skill with which the 3/10 Baluch Regiment has played its part since they came to us in April, 1942. In particular the great recovery brought about by that Battalion in its counter-attack in July last, on the Ruweisat Ridge, is a feat of arms that will ever be remembered by this Division.

"We wish the Battalion all good luck and a speedy return to the Division."

It was a charming tribute paid by one of the most distinguished generals which war had brought to eminence, but it was hard to say good-bye to the 5th Brigade. It was almost a gloomy battalion which detrained on the 14th of February at Cairo to take over garrison duties from the 1st/9th Gurkhas. Since its arrival in Basra in August, 1941, the Battalion had been switched about through many brigades and formations which, however exigent the circumstances controlling these matters, is a bad habit. To be relegated back to Cairo, under the direct notice and grasping paw of Supreme Headquarters, was a step in the wrong direction.

And so it proved. The Battalion carried out its garrison duties among the fleshpots of Cairo for a month or so, and then by another stroke of fate lost its identity as a battalion in a completely novel role. Before recounting this odd adventure the total casualties suffered by the Battalion for the year ending the 20th of April, 1943, should be recorded:

Officers

Captain R. K. Williams	Died
Captain Sardar Ali	Wounded
Lieutenant H. L. Frey	Prisoner of war
Lieutenant F. S. Panton	Prisoner of war

Viceroy's Commissioned Officers

Subadar Sultan Khan	Wounded
Subadar Gopi Chand	Wounded
Subadar Ghulam Mohd	Wounded
Jemadar Dharm Pal	Wounded
Jemadar Zaristan	Wounded

Other Ranks

Killed	22
Wounded	72
Wounded and prisoner of war	3
Missing	114

THE INVASION OF SICILY: APRIL TO AUGUST, 1943

Our new role, it seemed at first, was to be combatant dock labourers. The object of this transformation was a top secret. On the 15th of April Taylor had been summoned to a conference at General Headquarters, Middle East, and was informed that the 3rd Baluch and a Frontier Force battalion had been selected to provide working companies on the beaches for the future invasion of Europe. G.H.Q., sympathetically enough, tried to soften the blow by stressing the bright side of the picture. The companies—the only Indian troops being employed—would be landed in Europe within a few hours of the assault troops; they would probably be engaged in the mopping-up operations; in the event of a reverse they would have to defend the beach-head. The original intention had been to form working companies from the British reinforcements in the Middle East, but owing to casualties in Tripoli and Tunisia this had become impossible. Battle-experienced, disciplined troops, who would not be demoralized or shaken by bombing and ground strafing, were essential for the task. The 3rd Baluch were chosen.

After the shock had been absorbed the Battalion threw itself into the new work with its customary energy. Much reorganization had to be done to split the Battalion into five self-contained companies. These were numbered consecutively from No. 60 to No. 64, No. 60 Baluch Company being the old "A" Company, and personnel of H.Q. Company becoming No. 64 Baluch Company. The establishment of each company was two officers, three Viceroy's commissioned officers, a hundred and twelve other ranks and six followers. At the end of April these companies joined their new formations, which for security reasons necessary to conceal their function were called "Bricks." Nos. 60, 61 and 62 Companies joined No. 31 (Marine) Brick at Kabrit, and Nos. 63 and 64 joined No. 34 (Welch) Brick at Gaza, Palestine.

On joining these bricks the men found that, far from being relegated to pioneer fatigues, their new duties comprised work demanding high technical skill, sound tactics and weapon training, and physical fitness, all within the framework of a carefully planned organization, perfected by the War Office. Once again the Battalion was to go into secret training, but this time with the exciting prospect that Hitler's "impregnable fortress" was the goal. The war establishment of these bricks will show the complexity of organization which the growing science of combined operations demanded. The parent battalion of No. 31 (Marine) Brick was the 7th Battalion Royal Marines, who supplied one company of Marines and the administrative and training staffs. The component parts consisted of:

One Field Company, R.E.
One Heavy Battery, A.A.
One Light Battery, A.A.
No. 31 Beach Maintenance Centre (B.M.C.).

This beach maintenance centre had an establishment of fifty officers and nearly one thousand two hundred other ranks, of which our three companies formed part. The remaining personnel consisted of representatives of all British arms: gunners, Armoured Corps, Marines, Royal Air Force, Ordnance, transport and medical services.

At Kabrit and Gaza for the next two months these miscellaneous bodies of troops were welded into specialized, integrated units. Originally a British establishment, the arrival of Indian troops—with different messing arrangements, different equipment and, of course, language—in their midst called at first for some adjustments. The British officers and soldiers had little or no experience of Indian soldiers, and our appearance was at first greeted with some reserve. The ice was broken in No. 34 (Welch) Brick when "D" Company completed the obstacle course in seven and a half minutes, knocking six and a half minutes off the previous record. That performance induced respect, and within a few days cordial relations had been established. The Baluch companies had also the indefinable prestige of those who had fought in the Desert, an experience not yet shared by many of their fellow "brick-walas."

Training was hard. After some experimentation, field service marching order was stabilized at a seventy-pound load carried on the man. Each company could now move anywhere on its feet as a self-contained unit, freed from a baggage tail. Endurance marches with these loads were carried out. All companies had a week's course on the beaches, unloading craft, packing dumps, reloading into lorries, manipulating roller runways for the disembarkation of vehicles, rigging folding boats and the other varied equipment required for amphibian operations. Much time was spent on swarming up and down ropes, ladders and scrambling nets—a technique which few landlubbers understand—and in dashing into and out of assault boats with varying loads; also an exercise undreamt of in the philosophical recruiting areas of the Punjab.

Some new officers had arrived during the past six months. Battalion Headquarters, with Taylor, Lane and Van Loo, had moved from Cairo to Qassassin. Those left in executive command of the brick companies were:

No. 31 (Marine) Brick

No. 60 Company ("A" Company)
  Commander: Captain J. H. Nicholls.
  Second-in-Command: Lieutenant D. S. MacDonald.
  Platoon Commanders:
    Subadar Shara Khan.
    Jemadar Allah Ditta.
    Jemadar Ghulam Hussain.

No. 61 Company ("B" Company)
  Commander: Lieutenant Ali Bahadur.

Second-in-Command: Second-Lieutenant Janjua.
Platoon Commanders:
  Subadar Hassan Gul.
  Jemadar Abdul Wahab.
  Jemadar Sabr Aslar.

No. 62 Company ("C" Company)
Commander: Captain Sardar Ali.
Second-in-Command: Lieutenant B. J. Sutton.
Platoon Commanders:
  Subadar Kirpa Ram.
  Jemadar Walayat Ram.
  Jemadar Ram Dhan.

No. 63 Company ("D" Company)
Commander: Captain J. K. Chandy.
Second-in-Command: Second-Lieutenant R. J. W. Craig.
Platoon Commanders:
  Subadar Sultan Khan.
  Jemadar Gulistan.
  Jemadar Karjasab Khan.

No. 34 (WELCH) BRICK

No. 64 Company (H.Q. Company)
Commander: Captain V. H. Morley.
Second-in-Command: Lieutenant F. T. Lockwood.
Platoon Commanders:
  Subadar Bostan Khan.
  Jemadar Sat. Barg.
  Jemadar Rattan Chand.

LIAISON OFFICERS

Forster was appointed to the Marine Brick and Robinson to the Welch Brick.

These were the officers who carried out the whole training and operations with their bricks.

When this individual training had been completed more advanced work was practised in conjunction with the troops who were actually going to make landings. For instance, the Marine Brick had a full-scale operation across the Bitter Lake on the Suez Canal with its assault brigade at the end of May. Shortly afterwards the physical endurance of the men was thoroughly tested on the docks at Fanara, platoons working six hours on and twelve hours off for some days in the unloading of awkward stores. The target was six hundred tons per company in the twenty-four hours. The men treated this trivial burden lightly.

During the first fortnight of June all brick companies were engaged in a full-dress rehearsal in the Red Sea, transported in the liners *Strathnaver*, *Otranto* and *Orontes*, with all the relevant staff and troops taking part in the invasion on board. Rough seas delayed the programme, but eventually a suitable beach in the Gulf of Akaba was found and the exercise was practised with no incident. Living on board for ten days, the men found their sea-legs and were exercised in the necessary sea routines in the same ships which were to take them to Europe. So far, all training had been done on identical lines; we must now follow the individual fortunes of the two bricks on field service.

No. 31 (MARINE) BRICK

General Montgomery inspected the brick on the 12th of June and his comments on the Baluch companies were terse and characteristic: "A very smart lot." On the 25th of June he gave one of his renowned talks to all officers at Ataka, and the next day the briefing of company commanders took place. They saw models and air photographs of the still-undisclosed beaches for the first time, and were told the plan for the assault. On the 30th of June the three companies embarked in the *Strathnaver* at Suez. At Port Said the ship moored off Simon Artz, and the men were permitted to go ashore for a bathe. Early on the 5th of July the convoy sailed, twelve great liners escorted by ships of the Allied navies. The *Orontes*, with "D" and H.Q. Companies on board, took station on the starboard beam for the voyage. Except for one enemy plane which flew over, there was no enemy activity, and the invasion fleet grew into an armada, estimated at over two thousand four hundred craft. On the 8th of July the secret was divulged to all ranks that Sicily was the target, and the 10th of July D Day. Final rehearsals on the models ensured that every man knew his job, and it was with feelings of great excitement that the men saw the dark shape of Etna looming on the horizon on their last evening on board.

[The invasion force was the 15th Army Group under General Alexander (Deputy Commander-in-Chief to General Eisenhower), comprising the British Eighth Army under General Montgomery and the American Seventh Army under General Patton. Landings were made on a hundred-mile stretch of the south-east coast of Sicily.]

The beaches allotted to the 231st Infantry Brigade, with No. 31 (Marine) Brick in attendance, were two small coves lying some ten miles east of Sicily's most southern tip, the Pachino Peninsula. This was an independent landing between two divisional landings. The 1st Dorsets were to take Amber Beach on the right, the 1st Hampshires Red Beach on the left, with the 2nd Devons in reserve to land on either beach. Zero hour was at 0300 hrs., and the first assault wave got away from the liner without alarming the enemy. Success signals were soon observed, and although an enemy searchlight swept over and lit up the landing craft the defences were either blind or asleep. The 231st Brigade had only two men killed and twelve wounded. There was the occasional rattle of automatic fire heard between the sharp barks of the naval sloops cruising up and down blasting shore installations. By dawn the whole sea was crowded with myriads of landing craft ferrying men and guns ashore from the L.S.Is. which stood seven miles out to sea.

At 0629 hrs. the first Baluch party ("B" Company) left the *Strathnaver*, followed shortly afterwards by the other companies. By 1000 hrs. they were all ashore happily digging into Europe. The companies had been allotted the northern open flank of the beach, the place of honour, as it was from this quarter that the counter-attack was expected. The first two nights were spent in battle positions.

Much of the initial success of the landings was due to the way the enemy airfields had been paralysed by the Royal Air Force, the enemy being unable to get planes off the ground to repel the successive waves of Allied aircraft. Enemy air activity was confined to the first four days, on the first night a small raid being made on the stone quay of Marzamemi village, where Nos. 8 and 12 Platoons were unloading. The men took what shelter they could behind walls and in ditches. One heavy bomb killed the Brick Intelligence Officer and his sergeant and wounded two Baluchis, one badly. On the night of the 14th there was a spectacular raid in which some eight enemy aircraft came down in flames, one Ju.88 jettisoning its bombs on the edge of "B" Company area without damage. Throughout these night raids the bearing of the men was excellent: they were always under control and the first back to work.

These interruptions were only incidentals to the main job of unloading war material on Red and Amber Beaches, which went on day after day, six hours on and twelve hours off, for fourteen days. The tally of tonnage unloaded in this fortnight from landing craft on to open beaches, and stacked in appropriate areas, is impressive. On D Day three hundred and seventeen tons were unloaded. On D2 Day seven hundred and forty-eight tons. Thus it went on day after day with varying totals, ranging from a peak of one thousand five hundred and thirty-five tons on D4 to a mere two hundred and seventeen tons unloaded before breakfast on the 24th of July. Altogether, these three Baluch companies handled thirteen thousand three hundred and fifty tons. It is hardly surprising that at the end of these Herculean labours the Brick Commandant wrote to his other sub-units urging them to emulate the spirit of the Baluch companies in competence, turn-out and discipline. A pretty compliment.

The companies bivouacked in a vineyard; their rations were Indian composite rations; extra blankets and mosquito-nets were issued, and Ordnance were soon on the spot to replace clothing. Despite the dirty nature of the work, or perhaps because of it, the highest standards of turn-out and personal hygiene were enforced. The men were not allowed to forget that they were soldiers first and foremost.

On the 24th of July the beaches closed down, and guard duties on a prisoner-of-war cage, military dumps and the railway station were taken over. On Sunday, the 25th of July, the news that Mussolini, Dictator for twenty-one years, had resigned caused only ribald comment. During August the companies remained in this quiet backwater whilst the American Army swept round the west and north coasts and the Eighth Army battled its way through Catania to Messina. On the 17th of August Allied Headquarters announced: "The Eighth English Army and the Seventh American Army have joined forces in Messina, and all organized resistance has ceased on the island."

No. 34 (WELCH) BRICK

We have left "D" and H.Q. Companies sailing in the *Orontes* from Port Said on the 5th of July. After putting to sea the captain of the ship announced over the Tannoy system that Sicily was the objective of the expedition. An "information room" was opened with a lavish display of air photographs, intelligence summaries, guide books and a plaster model of the coast and hinterland. Plans and orders were issued and studied.

The immediate plan was the landing of one of the brigades of the 50th Division on a beach near Avola (a railway station half-way between the Pachino Peninsula and Syracuse on the south-west coast). The Brigade was to land at 0300 hrs. on the 10th of July, clear the beaches by first light, and then capture the heights overlooking the beach to prevent observed artillery fire. Little opposition was expected in the initial stages.

At dawn on the morning of D Day the companies had a grand-stand view of the operations from the decks of the *Orontes* standing well out to sea. Surprise was complete, and the landings were effected with the smoothness and rapidity of a peace-time exercise. Except for some spasmodic gun fire there was no incident as the brick went ashore shortly afterwards and established its complicated lay-out on the beach. Enemy reactions came in the shape of heavy air attacks—thirty Ju.88's at a time—but their principal targets were the shipping, including a hospital ship which was wantonly sunk. These raids continued for three days, but our companies incurred no casualties and carried on with their work. A little night sniping ceased abruptly when one of our patrols discovered the "hide" in the hills furnished with rifles and ammunition. By the 12th of July ten Sicilian towns, including Pachino and Syracuse, were in Allied hands.

On the 14th of July this particular beach was closed and the brick, less the Baluch companies, moved to Syracuse to assist in operating the port there. The companies remained to clear up the beach until the end of July, when they also went to Syracuse. There, until the 7th of August, they worked on heavy night shifts from 1900 hrs. to 0600 hrs., until relieved by pioneers. They were employed on garrison duties in and around Syracuse until Battalion Headquarters arrived from Egypt on the 26th of August, 1943, the second anniversary of the invasion of Persia.

In September the 3rd Baluch was re-formed again in Syracuse with all companies reporting back, fit and well, after a strange interlude. The Eighth Army was now in Italy, established on a forty-mile front, ten miles deep, round the big toe, and the advance was continuing.

CHAPTER ELEVEN

ITALY : 1943—1944

WHEN the Battalion concentrated at Syracuse in September, 1943, its officer strength increased from eleven or twelve who had seen service in the Desert to nineteen. For the tough fighting ahead they, and more, were necessary. Lane and Van Loo had vanished for the time being on staff employment. Hamid Khan had become Adjutant, Lieutenant B. J. Sutton Mechanical Transport Officer, and Captain R. E. Purcell Quartermaster. Taylor, Forster, Nicholls and Chandy were at their original posts. Other appointments were:

"C" Company.—Captain V. H. Morley.

H.Q. Company.—Captain B. Jackson.

Company Officers:
  Captain R. H. Brown.
  Lieutenant Ali Bahadur.
  Lieutenant F. Lockwood.
  Lieutenant Daljit Singh.
  Lieutenant Janjua.
  Lieutenant Hickenbotham.
  Lieutenant S. S. MacDonald.
  Lieutenant R. J. W. Craig.
  Lieutenant P. S. Mack.

The Medical Officer, Captain D. N. Vora, now an experienced campaigner, remained at his aid post, and Subadar Nasib Khan succeeded Ahmed Nur as Subadar-Major.

On the 8th of September (the day Italy made formal surrender) the Battalion moved to Messina, where it remained until the 18th of November. Messina was a pleasant place, duties being garrison and guards on prisoner-of-war cages. The men were quartered in an unfinished hospital close to the stadium, where there were splendid facilities for games, and the straits were only a stone's-throw away. 'Id was celebrated in traditional fashion in October after an interval of two years. Companies were struck off duties in turn and were exercised in company training in the excellent training areas to the north and south of the town. The local supplies were plentiful and good. The officers' mess was *de luxe,* a private villa on a cliff overlooking the straits, and staffed by an admirable Sicilian butler and cook, who added forgotten refinements to the service and food. It was an enjoyable period which set up officers and men for the harsh winter conditions they were shortly to undergo on the mainland.

The Battalion crossed the straits to Italy on the 18th of November, 1943, and moved to Taranto. For the next five months, during a very severe winter, they were stationed in Taranto, Bari on the east coast, Avigliano, and back to Bari again, the journey being accomplished in a snowstorm and blizzard which stranded all the vehicles. Guard duties and training under vile conditions were the order of the day and night. Just before Christmas Taylor was admitted to hospital with pneumonia and was gravely ill for some months. His natural toughness won through and early in April he was welcomed back to the Battalion. Subadar-Major Akbar Khan, a great and popular Pathan, returned from India to take over from Nasib Khan.

Several odd events occurred. Among the escaped Allied prisoners who kept seeping through from Northern Italy during the confusion which followed Italy's surrender was an old friend, Jemadar Ismail Khan. He had been captured in the break-out from Mersa Matruh in 1942. After his escape from a prison camp he joined forces with a gunner subaltern, and those two wandered down the length of Italy until they reached the battlefront near Cassino. There they spent an interesting few days in directing the guns of the Fifth Army with a shaving mirror. When they reached the American lines they were able further to present their hosts with information and targets. Another arrival was Lieutenant Panton, who had similarly been put "in the bag" in the retreat to El Alamein. He had managed to escape from his escort when actually being transferred to Germany, and had lived for several weeks with an hospitable Italian family. Forster and Chandy had the equivocal duty of being personal guards on the body of a diminutive Italian general suspected of being a war criminal. He had to be kept under personal observation day and night, asleep or awake, for some days; an inglorious and embarrassing business for all concerned. In March the men were considerably interested in a rainfall of pure mud at Bari. It was caused by volcanic substance blown from Vesuvius. To celebrate his award of the Order of British India the Subadar-Major gave a tea party in the Indian branch of the Y.M.C.A., and among his guests was Lieutenant-Colonel D. F. Dalton (now of the 3rd/1st Punjab), who had been Akbar Khan's company commander twelve years before.

These small incidents helped to mitigate the dullness of routine work in Bari and the impatience, which consumed all, to return to the front. Taylor, characteristically, kept plugging away at higher command for a move forward. The Battalion was now completely organized, fully equipped and trained for the new campaigning season about to open. It was furthermore acclimatized to the strange Italian scene and the Latin exuberance of the inhabitants.

A training team from the 8th Division had spent some days with the Battalion and had given instruction in the tactics which fighting in Italy required. The open ranges of the Desert had disappeared. Distance had now to be measured by hours rather than miles. Traffic was confined to a few highways. The countryside, swarming with vagrants, refugees and other displaced persons, including enemy agents, made secrecy of movement improbable and surprise, therefore, virtually impossible. The battle had to be fought the hard way, elemental hand-to-hand slogging.

Early in January, 1944, the 4th Indian Division had arrived in Italy after its Tunisian victories, and was holding a sector from somewhat east of Osogna to Guardiagrele, with the 10th Indian Division on its right extending to the sea at Ortona. The present role of these divisions on this the Adriatic front was holding, which in effect meant that the divisions kept the enemy in a continual state of "jitters" by raids, patrols and "cutting-out" parties. On the 18th/19th of April the Battalion moved from Bari, delighted to rejoin the 4th Indian Division, and by the 23rd of April had come under the command of Brigadier O. Lovett, in the 7th Brigade. The first battle position was on a lateral road north of Castelfrentano, with three companies forward and "D" Company in reserve. A few days in this area and then forward again to the Colle Bianco, a narrow ridge jutting south towards Guardiagrele, which overlooked it. "D" and "C" Companies took over the forward portion, with "A" Company in reserve, while "B" Company occupied a hamlet, Chiamato, three miles

COLONEL A. C. TAYLOR, D.S.O.
(Commandant, 1941-1944)

to the north-west, and came under the command of the 1st Royal Sussex in that sector.

The organization of patrols became the major task. Lieutenant Craig was appointed Battalion Patrolmaster, and with his staff lived in the forward sector, spying the land and learning the topography. The Germans were vigorous and offensive on the whole Indian front and clashes between patrols and raiding parties were of nightly occurrence. It was a hard school, but in it the new young drafts from India soon found their feet. There were some incidents the first weeks. The enemy made a night attack on "D" Company which held the most forward position. There were casualties on both sides before the Germans were driven back. On the night of the 5th of May Forster, in Chiamato, took out a patrol which captured intact a large wireless set and three German operators who were establishing an observation post in a farmhouse. The observation post's platoon escort (engaged in laying mines on the mule track by which "B" Company received its supplies) counter-attacked savagely, but were repulsed. Our casualties were Lance-Naiks Gul Badshah and Ayu Din killed, and one missing. Forster was subsequently awarded the Military Cross.

On the 7th of May, 1944, Lieutenant-Colonel A. C. Taylor, D.S.O., handed over command of the Battalion to Lieutenant-Colonel L. V. S. Sherwood, D.S.O., and went on leave to England. For three gruelling years Taylor had borne the heat and burden of the day, and throughout the amazing number of shifts and changes which the Battalion had undergone in its Middle East Odyssey he had remained at the helm, calm, determined, imperturbable, navigating the 3rd Baluch with great confidence and supreme competence through all the shoals and dangers which encompassed it. His departure grieved every man in the Battalion. Sherwood, however, made a splendid successor. He had spent all his service with the 4th Baluch, and in the earlier years of the war had distinguished himself in Eritrea and Keren. A great sportsman and athlete, he was just the right type of commandant required for the arduous physical toil and daring which the unfolding Italian campaign presented.

The 8th of May, 1944, marked the centenary of the Battalion. The Battalion was delighted to receive a telegram of congratulation and good wishes from Her Majesty Queen Mary. This was, however, hardly the time or place for any celebration. Most of "B" Company went out on a centenary patrol, but failed to find a quarry. [In about 1929 Maxwell, who was then Adjutant, suggested to the Commanding Officer (A. S. Auret) that it might be a wise provision to start a Centenary Fund. The proposal was accepted by all officers, who subscribed a small monthly amount to build up funds. The amount thus accumulated is now being employed to publish this History.]

For the next week there was activity on the whole of our front, the enemy probing into the defences of Chiamato and the Bianco Ridge, and being thrown back on both occasions by "B" and "D" Companies. In the meantime, there was heavy fighting on the whole Italian front. The Allied armies had assaulted the Gustav Line and by the 23rd of May the Adolf Hitler Line had been breached. The Allied left wing was on the move, and Supreme Headquarters was hopeful that the enemy on the Indian front would have to retreat to conform to the general withdrawal. To ascertain this possibility, the 3rd Baluch were ordered to carry out deep patrolling on their front and, in particular, to discover whether the enemy strong-point at Guardiagrele had been evacuated. Major Jackson, now commanding "B" Company, led one patrol, whilst two others, under Major R. H. Brown and Lieutenant Daljit Singh, were made up from H.Q. Company. These two patrols converged on the outskirts of Guardiagrele without incident, and decided to join forces and enter the town. There were no sentries in evidence, but suddenly on entering the town they were confronted with the somewhat alarming sight of hundreds of Germans engaged in the peaceful avocations of washing, cleaning cars and equipment, and other behind-the-line routine duties. Brown considered, reasonably enough, that his patrol had fulfilled its mission, and ordered a smart retreat. By this time the Germans had recovered their wits and the patrols had a nasty ordeal in fighting their way out again through heavy fire. Many individual acts of gallantry marked their progress back to a position where Jackson had established an observation post. Here he collected stragglers until he was also overrun. Our casualties were severe: Lieutenant Daljit Singh and Subadar Ram Dhan wounded, seven other ranks wounded, and twelve missing. Six of these were later confirmed as killed. Brown, who was reported as severely wounded and a prisoner, managed to get back the same day with nothing more painful than a sprained ankle. At about this time Major Hamid Khan left to attend a course at the Staff College.

A few days later the Battalion was moved to take over a sector on the 10th Division's front, and relieved the 3rd/1st Punjab opposite Crecchio. The position lay along the eastern bank of a nullah with the enemy on the western bank. The Germans had the advantage in that our sector was overlooked completely from the Colle di Tollo, a high feature only a thousand yards away. Three rifle companies were forward, with "C" Company in reserve. Any movement by day brought down immediate fire, and all reliefs were carried out at night. Patrolling became even more intensive. Each night, apart from routine protective patrols, at least three special patrols—an officers', an ambush and a fighting patrol—were on the prowl. The enemy was equally vigilant and came as close as he dared on several nights.

On the night of the 5th/6th of June the enemy appeared in strength on "D" Company's front, driving one of our fighting patrols—twenty-five Indian other ranks of "C" Company—before him. This party had gone out earlier under Lieutenant Hickenbotham. "D" Company was surrounded and the Germans tried to infiltrate towards "C" Company and Battalion Headquarters. The engagement lasted until 0500 hrs., when the enemy withdrew. Our casualties were nine, but from the evidence of prisoners it was learnt that the Germans had suffered much more heavily in this determined attack. Hickenbotham and one sepoy of his patrol were still missing.

On the 8th of June our scouts found that the enemy had withdrawn all along the line. This was the first intimation that the Division had of his intention. On advancing, the bodies of Lieutenant Hickenbotham and the missing sepoy were found together a short distance from their patrol's objective, to which this courageous young officer had led them. He was pressing home the attack with pistol and bomb in either hand when killed. As the Commanding Officer was conducting his burial service that morning, Lieutenant Ali Bahadur, who had been sent forward to clear a gap in the minefield, was blown up by an S-mine and killed.

The clearing of the minefield took some hours, but by the afternoon "A" and "C" Companies were pushing along the Tollo—Canosa road without, however, making contact with the enemy. The next day the 5th Brigade was recalled from the pursuit, and on the 14th of June the 4th Indian Division, of which the Battalion was now finally a definite unit, moved to Campo Basso for specialized training. These seven weeks of the Italian campaign had caused more casualties than El Alamein:

Killed.—Two officers, one Viceroy's commissioned officer and nineteen Indian other ranks.

Wounded.—One officer, one Viceroy's commissioned officer and thirty-eight Indian other ranks.

Missing.—Six Indian other ranks.

July, 1944, was a busy month. The weather was mostly sunny with brief patches of cloud and rain. The first week was spent in training, which included a Battalion rifle meeting, the second in continuous movement, often in bewildering directions, and the last fortnight in operations. The Battalion was up to strength again with an average of fourteen officers, nineteen Viceroy's commissioned officers and seven hundred and ten other ranks. The armament, now segregated in the Support Company, consisted of nineteen carriers, eight 6-pounder anti-tank guns, and a machine-gun platoon formed on the 8th of July under Subadar Bostan Khan. Major M. Forster was appointed Second-in-Command, *vice* Major J. F. Robinson, who was posted to our 4th Battalion, now also in the Italian theatre. Major T. P. Kidd joined the Battalion, and took over "C" Company.

Major operations in Italy, which had been checked until Cassino was overwhelmed on the 25th of May, had become fluid again. With the Liri Valley opened and Anzio relieved, the Fifth Army had driven on Rome and the Eighth Army was fanning out in pursuit through Central Italy. The Germans had made a withdrawal of some two hundred and fifty miles to their next "lay-back," the renowned Gothic Line. There they were working on a position of great natural strength on the Etruscan Apennine Massif.

On the 5th of July the 5th Brigade moved by road from Campo Basso to Rome, thence via Bastia, Andrea and San Vincenzo to the village of Monte San Maria, where it arrived on the 12th of July. The 4th Division's new location was the twenty miles or so of the watershed separating the Tiber and Arno Rivers in the north of Umbria. The countryside is beautiful in peace, but beastly in war. Well-wooded slopes, small rivers and ravines running to all points of the compass, stoutly built hamlets, each a strong-point, and sixteenth-century manor houses constructed to withstand a siege. It was the North-West Frontier over again, only this time against an enemy superbly equipped with all weapons for defence.

An extract from the Battalion's War Diary for one day is of interest, as it shows battle procedure in action:

"PLACE 541221.　　Date: 13 July, 1944.
Time 1000 hrs. Advance party move to recce new dispersal area.
1600 hrs. Recce party under C.O. move to Monte S. Maria.
1645 hrs. C and D coys move up to new dispersal area. Are shelled on the road. Captain Brown and 2 IORs wounded, and two IORs killed. Bn. concentrate in area 549258.
1900 hrs. 'R' Gp. (Reconnaissance Group) return to concentration area.
2000 hrs. C.O. gives out orders for a night attack.
2030 hrs. 'O' Gp. (Order Group) move up to M.S. Maria to a view point.
2045 hrs. Bn. moved up with the intention of proceeding to M.S. Maria. On arrival at 514276 orders were received that the operation was cancelled and the Bn. were to remain in present area."

San Maria was a picturesque village perched on a peak and occupied at this time by the Royal Sussex. Our Battalion was ordered to move through it and occupy the next ridge of Monte Cedrone, two miles farther north. It was to be a night attack based on the hopeful rumour that the enemy had evacuated the position. Before the Battalion had reached the start line of the River Erci enemy shelling stampeded the baggage and gun mules, and as a proper reconnaissance of the difficult ground had not been possible the Higher Command cancelled the attack. (On the following night the 10th Brigade, consisting of the Durham Light Infantry, 4th Baluch and 2nd/4th Gurkhas, supported by two hundred guns, broke through the Uppiano positions and captured the ridge.)

The Battalion now concentrated at San Maria, where Foster celebrated his promotion by commanding a two-company raid on Cagnano. Until the 20th of July vigorous patrolling was carried out to discover the enemy strong-points. The 4th Division was then pulled out of this sector and moved to positions in front of the town of Arezzo, where the Battalion had one day's rest before its next commitment.

This was spectacular. On the night of the 24th of July the 5th Brigade made a daring advance well into the enemy's position. The 3rd Baluch's objective was Point 677, some six miles ahead, the route being across a broad enclosed valley and climbing a precipitous slope densely covered with scrub. It was a completely successful attack. At dawn the Battalion reached the summit and the enemy were so surprised that they fled, leaving their medium machine guns and mortars as booty. Counter-attacks were repulsed, but any further advance on the left front was opposed by accurate shelling. For his leadership on this occasion Major Kidd won the Military Cross. That night the Essex passed through to join up with the 10th Division in the east. This brigade advance effectively sealed off several enemy formations in a narrow salient between the two Indian divisions, and the intervening sector was cleared without further fighting. Thus July finished satisfactorily. Major Lane rejoined.

August on the whole was a month of sunshine with some mountain rainstorms to lay the dust, and every day, with few exceptions, was spent arduously. To gain more elbow-room the 4th Division now wheeled west, and began to probe the ridge system of Prato Magno, the steep range running south-east between Florence and Arezzo. Speed was the watchword of this movement, the purpose of which was to outflank and encircle enemy outposts and strong-points covering the Gothic Line, whose main defences followed the crests of the High Apennines.

At nightfall on the 1st of August the Battalion moved to a bivouac area in the village of Scille, and at dawn moved by bounds over a series of hill features, meeting no opposition until 1000 hrs., when "A" Company (Major Sardar Ali) ran into enemy resistance on the final objective. This was rapidly reduced and the line established. Heavy shelling followed, one dump of mortar ammunition near Battalion Headquarters being set on fire. It was extinguished without serious damage. During the patrolling which continued for the next few days "B" Company found three British civilians living in a house in no-man's-land.

The 4th Division's operation was progressing satisfactorily, and all appeared set for the assault on the Gothic Line proper; but Allied Headquarters had decided to make the main attack not on the east flank but to the west. Accordingly, early in August the 4th Division was switched with the utmost secrecy from the Arno Valley across Italy via Lake Trasimeno. All identification marks were removed from men and vehicles, leaving only the Essex in their original area to display their Red Eagles and deceive the enemy. Unaware of the real purpose behind this move, the Battalion found itself near Perugia, a delightful place where it was vainly imagined a halt for rest and refit would ensue. Short leave was opened for visits to Rome and other places of interest.

Despite the beauty of the scenery the country traversed was full of danger. For instance, the 9th of August may be cited as an unlucky day. At 1000 hrs. a three-ton lorry exploded a mine. At 1245 hrs., when "D" Company was unloading kit, an ammunition mule, loaded, examined a cornstook which the retreating Germans had laced with a box mine. The subsequent explosion killed two men of the Mule Company and wounded one Viceroy's commissioned officer and fourteen Indian other ranks of "D" Company. At 1500 hrs., when "B" Company was unpriming grenades, one exploded and wounded five sepoys. Hidden booby traps lurked everywhere, and there was cruel evidence in the villages that Nazi formations were wreaking vengeance on hapless men and women.

In the meantime the Eighth Army was putting the final touches to its preparations for its mighty thrust on the eastern end of the Gothic Line. The 4th Division was assembled north of the town of Gubbio, which lay some thirty-five miles south of the Eighth Army's left flank. The Division's task was to push through rapidly to its battle positions and to go over to the attack immediately without waiting for zero hour on the remainder of the British front. This was intended to be a left hook at the enemy's jaw—to distract his attention.

The 5th Brigade moved across country and, meeting only minor opposition, had travelled seventy miles (as the crow flies) over villainous mountains between the 23rd and 29th of August. The Battalion was on the lightest scale possible with mule transport, and foot-slogged the whole way. Crossing the Mataure River the 5th and 7th Brigades joined hands to enter Urbino, where twenty thousand inhabitants greeted the sepoys with tumult and rapture. The Battalion pushed on to occupy the Pallino Ridge.

In front lay the Foglia Valley and, beyond the river, the high ridges which hid the outworks of the Gothic Line. *L'audace, toujours l'audace* was the spirit which animated all the battalions of the fighting 5th Brigade. Patrols reported that the Foglia was only lightly held, and that night "A" Company (Sardar Ali), supported by Sherman tanks, crossed the river, climbed the ridge and seized Monte della Croce, a hamlet overlooking the valley. Owing to a muddle between the German formations in this sector, the responsibility for this flank had not been clearly defined. Not a shot was fired, but by dawn the enemy's reactions were violent. He launched several counter-attacks under heavy artillery support, dislodging one of "A" Company's platoons, but "D" Company arrived in time to restore the position. In the bitter fighting which ensued two Viceroy's commissioned officers (Jemadars Ghulam Hussain and Abuza Khan) were killed, and Subadar Munsif Khan, second-in-command of "A" Company, later died of wounds.

During the night of the 30th of August the other rifle companies arrived, and under Major Lane's direction Monte Croce was firmly consolidated. It was with pardonable pride that the Battalion learnt that this was the first breach of the Gothic Line on the whole front. Major Sardar Ali was awarded the Military Cross, and the Army Commander sent Sherwood a congratulatory signal complimenting the 3rd Baluch on its achievement. On the following night the main assault by the Eighth Army opened up on a fifteen-mile front with a terrific barrage. The 5th Brigade's objective was Monte Calvo, and the three battalions, with tank support, were engaged in heavy fighting all day. Enemy medium machine-gun nests, mines and Spandaus held up "C" Company in a frontal attack, but by nightfall one platoon of "D" Company, with tanks, fought its way into the village and captured some forty prisoners. Our casualties in these past two days of August were: killed, three Viceroy's commissioned officers and nine Indian other ranks; wounded, two Viceroy's commissioned officers and fifty-eight Indian other ranks.

The first few days of September were spent in defensive positions around Monte Calvo. Desultory shelling and mortaring inflicted a few more casualties, but drafts from India soon had the Battalion up to full strength again. The 4th Indian Division had made good progress on its front despite the Germans' quick recovery from the confusion of the initial assault, and by the 5th of September the three brigades were facing the Pian di Castello Ridge beyond the Ventano River. On the 9th of September the Battalion took over positions on this ridge from elements of the 2nd/7th Gurkhas and 3rd/12th Frontier Force Regiment, and the next few days were spent in reconnaissances and preparations for an attack on the Gemmano Ridge.

Five battalions had already tried to take this particularly dour strong-point and had failed. The weather had broken and pelting rain had turned the fields into bogs and the mountain paths into mud-slides. Sherwood's plan was for a night attack, "C" Company to move from the start line at 2000 hrs. for the first objective, with "A" Company to pass through and on to the second objective. By 2330 hrs. "A" Company was on its objective and digging in when the enemy counter-attacked. "B" Company, on its way to the third objective, got involved in this severe hand-to-hand fighting, and, although "A" Company had to give ground, "B" managed to fight its way through in the darkness, and by dawn had a precarious hold on Gemmano. A splendid performance by all concerned. Major Lane was in command and held on grimly throughout the day with "B" Company and one platoon of "C." The following night the company was withdrawn. For his gallant leadership on this occasion Lane was awarded the Military Cross. The British 46th Division on the right made eleven attacks on Gemmano, each time to be thwarted by a desperate defence. Eventually Gemmano was captured on the 15th of September by the 4th Indian Division in a fully mounted attack supported by two hundred and sixty guns. The enemy lost over nine hundred killed in defending these few acres of high ground surrounding the village, which marked some of the toughest fighting of the whole campaign. In this final assault the Camerons played a leading and spectacular part.

On the 16th of September the Battalion put in a successful attack to the west of Taverno. On the following evening two fighting patrols, under Subadar Kirpa Ram of "C" Company and Lieutenant Craig of "D" Company, slipped across the Merano River into San Marino State. During the night both these companies established bridgeheads against opposition across the river at Faetano. The 1st/9th Gurkhas passed through and engaged the enemy in a sanguinary clash on the high ground beyond. The remainder of the Brigade came through and on the 21st the Divisional Commander (Holworthy) and the 5th Brigade Commander (Saunders-Jacob) drove into San Marino in jeeps and were entertained by the Captain Regent in his palace. The Battalion bivouacked under the shelter of San Marino—its cliff sides crowned by spires and towers—and came into divisional reserve. During the past thirty-five days the Division had advanced over sixty miles, the last twenty-five miles through a defensive zone heavily massed by first-line troops with a great weight of artillery and armour in support. Although the broken weather, with its rains, gales and bitter cold, had slowed down the offensive, the spirits of the men were happy and confident. During September our total casualties were twelve Indian other ranks killed and sixty-one wounded.

Early in October the Division was moved back to Umbria to rest in the Perugia area, and the men were billeted in houses, a forgotten luxury. On the way back contact was made with our 4th Battalion, and the men spent a whole day in entertaining each other. For the next few weeks individual training and short leave occupied the men's attention, while speculation centred on the date the Division would be recalled to the front for the final overthrow of the enemy. That was not to be.

Orders came for the 4th Indian Division to move to Taranto for embarkation to Greece, which was about to be liberated. A new phase of operations was opening up in a new country, but to the hardened campaigners of the Battalion—now inured to any change of policy, plan, terrain or enemy which this strange war might produce—the prospect was merely another day's work.

At this point a considerable reshuffling of officers took place. Among those who left were Captains Morley and Purcell, who had been Quartermaster for most of the Italian campaign. The newcomers included:

    Major P. S. Hunt.
    Major K. J. F. Nailor.
    Major P. E. Jackson.
    Captain Hamid Khan.
    Captain T. M. Creasy.
    Captain H. H. Marsden.
    Lieutenant Mohd Anwar Khan.
    Lieutenant Hamid-ur-Rehman.

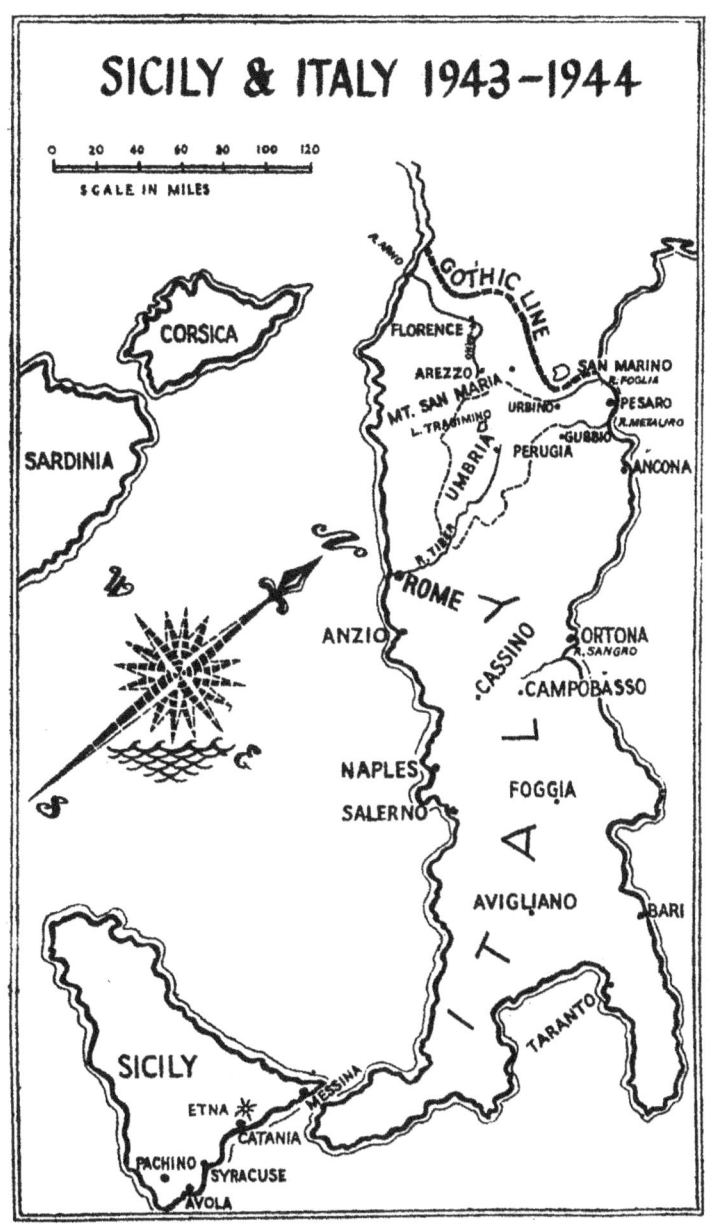

CHAPTER TWELVE

GREECE: 1944—1946

DURING the German occupation of Greece the fissiparous tendencies of its political groups, of which there were thirty-nine, appeared to coalesce into two main factions, ELAS and EDES. ELAS was the left-wing, anti-monarchy party and EDES the right-wing and pro-monarchy. There were, of course, other independent factions, some who actively assisted the Germans and others who used the uneasy period of Nazi rule to fight out their own private quarrels as guerrillas, bandits and outlaws. In September, 1944, when a German collapse seemed imminent, a conference was held at Caserta, near Naples, which was attended by the leaders of both ELAS and EDES, who were flown over for the meeting. They agreed to sink their differences and to accept the orders of the Allied High Command of the occupation forces during the liberation of Greece. Thereafter they agreed to obey the orders of the Greek Provisional Government until a free general election of the Greek people should decide the ultimate form of government.

In pursuance of this agreement two British brigades landed in Athens in mid-October, 1944, followed shortly afterwards by the Greek Prime Minister and his Provisional Government. Early in November Salonika, the principal port of Macedonia, was occupied also. The troops received an hysterical welcome from all factions whenever they appeared, and at first matters went well. In Macedonia ELAS had established a rough-and-ready form of administration, and their ambitious leaders were making every effort to spread their influence over the rest of Greece. ELAS were predominant in strength, organization and arms, and controlled all major offices of administration. Their political opponents got short shrift. Clashes between ELAS and EDES bands became more frequent.

ELAS, frightened that the Provisional Government would summon the King of the Hellenes to be a rallying-point for all anti-Communist and anti-Socialist Greeks, decided in November to make Athens the scene of a trial of strength, and began to infiltrate its forces into the capital. On the 3rd of December the ELAS members of the Provisional Government resigned, and a general strike—the usual Communist tactic—was declared. Following a day of street fighting with the police, ELAS on the 4th of December attacked the British and Greek Naval Headquarters in Piræus, the port of Athens. The British Commander, General Scobie, ordered all ELAS formations to leave the city by the 7th of December, under penalty of being declared hostile.

On the 8th of December, 1944, the 4th Indian Division sailed from Italy and the 5th Brigade was diverted from its original objective, the Ægean Islands, to Piræus. The Brigade (1st/4th Essex, 1st/9th Gurkhas and 3rd Baluch) landed on the night of the 11th/12th of December, and the remainder of the month was spent in bloody street fighting. The ELAS forces had mortars and machine guns, and knew the ground. An extract from the War Diary for the 16th of December will help to illustrate these arduous operations:

> "0230 hours. Orders received from Bde. Comd. that 2 Coys. 1/9 Gurkhas held up on Road Ifaistou and that 3 Baluch will clear blocks 1—6 and North to Ifaistou.
> 0400 hours. Orders issued that D coy. will clear blocks 1—6 by 0930 hours. B coy. will then pass through and clear remaining blocks and will then form cordon on road Ifaistou. D coy. will be in reserve until A and C coys. have reached objective, and will then take over from them and form cordon. A and C coys. being in reserve.
> 1115 hours. Coy. sent to Limin Zeas to search all boats landing from south.
> 1200 hours. Main H.Qs. move to house, 36, south of Limin Zeas.
> 1250 hours. C coy. on objective. 2 casualties.
> 1450 hours. A coy. on objective.
> 1600 hours. B coy. on objective.
> 1800 hours. Orders given out for 17th December operation. Battalion will advance as far as railway on a 4 coy. front."

And so it went on day after day. It is a relief to record this extract of an event which occurred on the afternoon of the 20th of December: "Greek demonstrations outside Battalion H.Qs. cheered Union Jack, played National Anthem, and a delegation gave a vote of thanks to the Colonel. Battalion under sporadic mortar fire all day." On the night of the 22nd/23rd of December the Brigade crossed the harbour and landed on the quays of Dhrapetsona in the northern harbour, and for several days was engaged in fierce but sporadic fighting. Rocket-firing aircraft and tanks were in support and did much to discourage the defenders. By the 1st of January, 1945, the Piræus dock, power and petrol installations had been recovered and a thousand prisoners taken by the Brigade. The Battalion's casualties in this ugly fighting were ten Indian other ranks killed, and two Viceroy's commissioned officers and fifty-four Indian other ranks wounded. Sherwood now took temporary command of the Brigade, and Major T. P. Kidd, M.C., the Battalion.

On the 15th of January, 1945, a truce was concluded in Athens, by the terms of which ELAS undertook to withdraw from the capital and Salonika, and to occupy rural concentration areas. The phase of active operations had ended, and the role of the 4th Indian Division became tutelary rather than bellicose. On the day before the armistice the 5th Brigade sailed from Piræus to Volos, an important port on the east coast. The role of the Battalion was simple: "To maintain law and order and prevent ELAS elements from beating up friendly Greeks."

Despite the truce, ELAS malcontents continued to act treacherously, and needed careful watching. Patrols were sent out to the villages, where they generally received splendid welcomes, but at the same time there was an undercurrent of hostility, kept murmuring by agitators, which made the distinction of friend or foe difficult, especially for the sepoys, unaccustomed to the primitive hatreds of Greek politics. As an example, on the 23rd of January, four civilians approached a platoon post of "B" Company. When challenged by the sentry they threw two grenades at him and fired with tommy-guns. The platoon shot back at them with no reported casualties on either side.

In February, a wet and cloudy month, the same strenuous work continued. On the 14th of February a larger operation was staged when the Battalion carriers and a squadron of the Central India Horse were sent to Heraidia to stop fighting between four hundred ELAS and a hundred Nationalists, a mission successfully completed in two days. On the 25th of February orders were received for the Battalion to move to Larissa, where ELAS formations were being concentrated. This move, however, did not prevent Major W. H. M. Lane, M.C., from being married to Miss Wetherell in Athens the same day. "Boomer" Lane and Forster were the two longest-service officers in the Battalion, and his marriage brought him the most cordial wishes from every officer and man in the 3rd Baluch.

By this time Greek National Guard battalions were being formed to take over the duties of law and order from the Allied forces, and Forster organized the Brigade Training School. They were difficult pupils, as their impartiality was always suspect. In a country riven by private vendettas and infectious partisan feeling it was an uphill task to persuade these newly recruited battalions that British methods of arrest and fair trial were preferable to the local methods of private vengeance and summary punishment. On the 2nd of March Kidd, with "A" Company, followed by a National Guard battalion, marched through Larissa to attend a civic reception. An ELAS sniper fired at the National Guards, who returned the fire, killing one and wounding seven civilians. The same day "A" Company took over large quantities of ELAS equipment, arms, animals and vehicles. The next ten days were spent by the Battalion in patrolling, searching and training the National Guards.

On the 17th of March orders were received for the 5th Brigade to move north into Macedonia. This northern province of Greece, bordered by Bulgaria, Yugoslavia and Albania, was the most turbulent and dangerous in the whole country. ELAS, often assisted by roving Germans, Italians, Bulgarians and Yugoslavs, were in a position of some strength which they were trying to consolidate and extend. In this tangled, backward province, with its extraordinarily miscegenated inhabitants—descendants of Macedonian Greeks, Osmanli Turks and Slavs—the Battalion was to spend its last year overseas. Events in Europe and Burma were approaching a victorious climax, and most officers and men would have preferred the straightforward fighting in those theatres to the anxious and devious problems which confronted them day and night in Northern Greece.

The journey from Larissa to Florina in Macedonia over mountainous roads in villainous condition was completed by the 20th of March, and patrols and exploratory parties were sent out in all directions to examine the attitude of the inhabitants. In almost all cases they had a friendly reception. By the end of the month the Battalion, now again under Sherwood's command, had reached its permanent station, the town of Veroia, about fifty miles west of Salonika. Battalion Headquarters and H.Q., Support and "D" Companies occupied the infantry barracks. "A" and "C" Companies were posted to the industrial town of Naoussa, twelve miles away, and "B" Company were sent to the village of Katerina, under the shadow of Mount Olympus, about forty miles to the north. The Brigade area of control extended over some one thousand eight hundred square miles.

The main object of the occupation was to bring peace and security to one of the most convulsed parts of Greece. This was carried out in three ways: firstly, by establishing a system of frontier control to prevent disruptive elements from entering the country; secondly, by hunting and arresting the collaborators of the German regime and the criminals of the ELAS terrorist organization; and, thirdly, by searching for and unearthing the large dumps of arms and ammunition, both German and British, which the Resistance Movement had hidden for use after the war. Companies were in most instances linked to companies of the National Guard and combined raids and patrols were carried out on villages suspected of harbouring criminals and concealing weapons. The National Guard carried out the actual searches and made the arrests, with the Allied forces standing by in support and to ensure fair play.

It should be realized that officers' responsibilities did not end with these operational commitments. The main task, indeed the principal object, was to nurse back into convalescence the sick body of Greek administration, which was almost moribund. Company and platoon commanders, in the guise of benevolent despots, had to see to the proper administration of justice, the encouragement of agriculture, the settlement of industrial disputes, the sanitation and health services of towns and villages, and, finally, to the equitable distribution of UNRRA supplies.

We have seen in this History how the Battalion on two occasions in Burma had carried out similar beneficent work in a country terrorized by dacoits, when duties and responsibilities were shouldered by the junior commanders out of all proportion to their rank and status. In comparison these were puny occasions, as the Macedonian situation was developing into a racial cockpit where all the New World ideologies were finding a stamping ground. By a curious freak of history the descendants of those very races—Pathan, Punjabi and Dogra—whom Alexander of Macedon subdued over two thousand years before, were to return to his country to try to bring civilization and peace. Tact, patience and strict impartiality were the prime essentials for the success of Allied policy, the restoration of freedom from want and fear.

For the first half of April strong patrols sent out for one or two nights at a time in conjunction with National Guards to search villages were unlucky; but it became apparent that their appearance in towns and villages was giving rise to confidence and trust, for by the end of April these patrols never returned empty-handed. During this fortnight these search parties brought back the following weapons and ammunition from widely separated hide-outs: two hundred and twenty-five thousand rounds of small-arms ammunition, sixteen thousand four hundred mortar bombs, a hundred and fifty-two grenades, twenty-six 75-mm. shells, twenty-five 25-pounder shells, four hundred and ninety-one rifles, thirteen machine guns, thirteen Sten guns and three tons of Teller mines.

ELAS supporters viewed this process of disarmament with annoyance, expressed often in the streets by rude remarks and ruder diatribes in their newspapers, but to these the men were impervious. An armed band tried to murder the Mayor of Neokhstron and fresh graves of ELAS victims were found in villages, but arrests in all cases were made and the suspects brought to trial. In this month, also, leave to India and England was opened and a large draft of three Viceroy's commissioned officers and seventy-eight Indian other ranks was sent to India. Sherwood also took sixty-one days to the United Kingdom, and Forster assumed command in the absence of Kidd, on a course in Italy. Training in the form of close-order battalion drill was started again, and at one of these parades the Brigade Commander pinned the decorations of the Military Cross on Lieutenant Craig and the two young jemadars, Sakhi Mohd and Kaka Ram, three fine distinctions awarded for gallantry in street fighting in Athens.

In May and June, with the weather growing more sultry, the roads more dusty and the mosquitoes more clamorous, the same type of work continued, with some variations. A Victory Parade on the 9th of May was only a transient interlude. A mixed bag of collaborators, murderers and Italian deserters, totalling eighty-three persons, was collected. Some of these showed fight and had to be disarmed. These raids were generally combined operations with the National Guard, but in some cases they were purely Battalion affairs to investigate reports of civilians being brutally molested by the National Guards themselves. For instance, Major Jackson was kept busy chasing a Corporal Costas, a National Guard deserter, who with an armed band was creating alarm and despondency in the Meliki area. The search for hidden arms had great success: a total of one hundred thousand rounds of small-arms ammunition, ninety-nine rifles, seventy grenades, fifty-seven machine guns, four pistols, eleven Sten guns, thirteen Teller mines and two thousand four hundred and sixty-two 75-mm. shells. One of the dumps was found in a church of the Greek Orthodox foundation.

Eminent visitors to Veroia included General Sir Claud Auchinleck, Commander-in-Chief, India, who spent a morning with the Battalion and addressed all ranks; and the Imam Sahib, the leading divine of the Juma Musjid, Delhi, who was deeply interested in the work of pacification. Minor works included the repair of bridges, the distribution of locust poison, and the arrest of the leaders of a KKE (Communist) unauthorized political meeting in Naoussa, where two thousand workers had been discharged from the cloth mills. Four officers, Craig, Creasy, Archer and Moncrieff, the last three being comparatively newcomers to the Battalion, went on leave to England.

In July a more than ordinary raid was arranged to round up some armed ELAS bands harassing villages in the marshes of the Yiannitsa district. Major P. E. Jackson was in command of a mixed force consisting of "C" and "D" Companies (less one platoon each), the Carrier Platoon, under Hamid Khan, a company of the National Guard, two sloops of the Greek Navy and two Royal Air Force machines. The plan was on the lines of a tiger shoot: the sea exits to be blocked by the naval vessels acting as "stops" whilst the carriers patrolled the river banks as wing "stops," and the three companies to sweep forward at first light in extended order in the role of beaters. It had the important difference that in this case the "beaters" were empowered to shoot if resisted. The operation was successful, twenty-five suspects being rounded up, and the "shikaris" returned to base at noon.

The strength of the Battalion now reached nine hundred all ranks, which allowed a large draft of four Viceroy's commissioned officers and a hundred and twenty-one Indian other ranks to go on leave to India. During these months changes among officers were frequent as the leave roster began to function on almost peace-time lines. Sherwood returned from England. and shortly afterwards Kidd went home on leave. In August a village raid by "A" Company under Lieutenant Mohd Anwar Khan yielded handsome prizes. The National Guard deserter, Corporal Costas, and his five desperado colleagues were captured with a small arsenal of weapons and ammunition. During this month armed bands of Yugoslavs and Bulgarians were reported in many areas, and drastic action was taken to round up their supporters and sources of supply.

The 15th of August, 1945, was declared the official end of the war, and another Victory Parade a few days later was only a slight interruption in the ceaseless programme of patrols, raids, cordons and administrative duties. Victory indeed seemed almost a mockery to the hard-pressed sepoys who had left India four years ago and saw around them only strife and instability.

On Sunday evening, the 2nd of September, 1945, a grim tragedy overtook the Battalion. A young sepoy, who had joined only three weeks before, murdered Lieutenant-Colonel L. V. S. Sherwood, D.S.O. (with bar), and Subadar-Major Akbar Khan, Sardar Bahadur, O.B.I. The murderer, a Punjabi Musulman from the Mianwali district, was found to be a religious fanatic. For an imagined grievance he shot these two great officers as they were seated in a jeep, and then gave himself up at the quarter guard. Tragedies of this nature are fortunately rare in the Indian Army, and are almost unknown among Punjabi Musulmans. This fact only intensified the horror and shame which filled the hearts of all ranks.

To ameliorate this sorrow, Forster, who now assumed command, decided that hard work was the cure, and day after day patrols sped over the hinterland of Macedonia rounding up suspects, investigating, searching and, above all, trying to solve the riddle of Greek unity. A large quantity of mines and dynamite charges was found, and several Yugoslav spies found and deported. In Naoussa six textile factories were on strike for a fifty per cent. increase in wages. To promote some sort of co-operation there an all-party conference was held to arrange VJ Day celebrations, but this fell through owing to mutual hostility, and tension only increased when ELAS and EAM decided to stage an illegal celebration.

Major K. J. F. Nailor, commanding "B" Company, carried out a raid on the village of Palaifiton on the night of the 1st/2nd of October. The village consisted of some three hundred houses, of which eighty were Nationalist and the remainder Communist. An informer had reported that eight Nationalist house-owners possessed illegal weapons, and the raid was arranged to collect these arms. Nailor, the force commander, describes the operation graphically and humorously in his official report:

"The raiding force left Naoussa on time. There was no moon and the night exceptionally dark. On arrival at Skidhera it was discovered that the other informers who were to meet the parties had grown tired of waiting and gone home. The force arrived on the main road opposite Palaifiton about four hundred yards from the village itself, and debussed.

"The parties were formed up in column, the idea being for the one remaining informer to lead the column rapidly through the village, dropping off parties at their respective houses. This was carried out successfully and complete silence maintained except for the local dogs barking and the force commander, who fell down a huge ditch while looking over his shoulder.

"When all parties had been positioned the 2-inch mortar fired a parachute flare. The bomb left the mortar successfully but returned to earth after a decent interval with a sickening thud—and in complete darkness. The second bomb was equally undemonstrative. The third, however, fulfilled its function as a source of light.

"Shortly afterwards three shots were heard from the area being searched by No. 6 Party. The force commander went to investigate and was told that as soon as the house was surrounded and the gendarmerie had demanded admittance a shot had been fired from a window. Two further shots had been fired, each from a different window. The party commander, Lance-Naik Mira Khan, was not certain whether the shots were fired by more than one rifle or whether the owner of the house was conducting a one-man all-round defence.

"The force commander approached the house with an interpreter and gendarme sergeant—carefully avoiding all windows. Through the interpreter the owner was told that there was a British force surrounding his house; that he would be charged with illegally possessing a firearm; and that if he succeeded in killing anybody he would also be charged with murder. The gendarme sergeant also encouraged the man to come out with his hands above his head.

"The answer came back from inside the house: 'I know you are "andartes" and have come to cut my throat, but you can't fool me with words. I have a grenade which I intend to throw at you if you don't go away.'

"This was followed by a shot from a door which the force commander had stupidly failed to notice on his approach to the house. However, the night was still very dark and the owner of the house a reasonably poor shot. It then sounded as if at least twenty females were having hysterics inside the house, whereupon it was decided not to force an entry at night for fear of hurting any innocent member of the household.

"The party, reinforced by another which had finished its job, took up positions round the house and prepared to wait for dawn, some three hours away. During that time some four more shots were fired, but no one was hurt. (In the meantime the other parties had carried out successful raids, discovering three pistols and a rifle.)

"Dawn and the headman of the village appeared together. Once again a party, consisting of the headman, the force commander, the gendarme sergeant and the interpreter, approached the house from which the firing had come. The situation was again explained to the owner, who at once came out, handed over his rifle and grenade, and apologized profusely for firing on Imperial troops. He was quite certain that the troops were 'andartes' come to kill him. He loved England.

"The bag of prisoners, numbering some thirty-four, were then interrogated. All were released except the five owners of the firearms. The crowd then saw the informer. This was an accident, but during the excitement no orders had been given for him to be hidden in the waiting transport while it was still dark. Before they could be stopped, several people set upon the informer. They were dispersed by Imperial troops.

"An orderly deputation then approached the force commander and said that the informer had been a well-known criminal. His son, at present hiding in the mountains, had killed four members of the village. The gendarme sergeant asked permission to arrest the informer pending further inquiries. This was given. The same deputation then asked for gendarmes to be sent from ————, as they feared reprisals. This was done and the raiding force left at 0815 hrs."

It would be tedious to describe all the raids of a similar pattern which were carried out in the last few months of the year. In spite of the incessant demand for patrols all through the summer, Sherwood, Kidd and Forster had been taking every opportunity of improving the standard of ceremonial and close-order drill. Whenever a few companies could be collected in Veroia, a ceremonial parade was practised with emphasis being laid on immaculate turn-out and precise drill movements. This bore great results in morale, smartness and pride of appearance, without which a soldier is nothing.

When the British Commander in Greece, General Scobie, came to Veroia early in October he was so impressed by the guard of honour found by the Battalion that a week later orders came for the 3rd Baluch to provide the ceremonial guards on Legation and Corps Headquarters in Athens. An inter-company drill competition was held to decide which companies should be selected for the honour, and "C" (Dogras) and "D" (Punjabi Musulmans) were chosen. Major P. E. Jackson commanded the detachment in Athens for November and December. Kidd returned from leave in England and Hamid Khan from India, bringing with him the new Subadar-Major, Shahra Khan, who had also been on leave.

Throughout the winter the distribution of UNRRA supplies was a major task. The supplies themselves were often short of the scheduled scale, and after distribution to those who were deemed responsible officials the Battalion was plagued with the investigation of charges and counter-charges of theft, corruption and black marketing. Six weeks before Christmas seven thousand Red Cross parcels were received for distribution to the poor and needy in the Battalion area. Forster took upon himself the distribution of two thousand five hundred parcels in Veroia, Major Sutton handed out one thousand seven hundred in Naoussa, and the remainder were taken by patrols to the surrounding villages. While these benevolent activities were being pursued, strikes, demonstrations, murders and assaults continued in the two

THE OFFICERS, 1946

(Photo taken in India shortly after the Battalion's arrival from Greece)

towns, but in all cases the appearance of our men in the troubled areas had an immediate tranquillizing effect, invariably without having to use force.

It is pleasant to record that the decent law-abiding citizens appreciated the work of the Battalion in an unusual manner. At a civic reception in Veroia Lieutenant-Colonel Kidd and Major Forster were presented with the freedom of the city. In presenting the two beautifully engraved parchment scrolls the Greeks gave full vent to their natural love of pageantry and goodwill, and, it is related, the wine of the country, oyzo, flowed freely. This happy ceremony set the seal on the Battalion's success in Macedonia.

Early in January, 1946, Subadar-Major Shahra Khan was summoned to Athens to be presented by the American Ambassador with the Bronze Star Medal, another signal tribute to the 3rd Baluch's good name. A week later the Divisional Commander inspected the Battalion and was singularly appreciative. On the 19th of January the joyful news came that the Battalion was to return to India in February. The announcement was received with tremendous satisfaction. Having handed over the area to the 2nd King's Regiment, the Battalion embarked at Salonika on the 17th of February, 1946, in the s.s. *Ruyes*, and arrived at its birthplace, Karachi, on the 28th of February. Queen Mary's Own was accorded a magnificent reception by the whole population.

The officers serving with the Battalion on its return from overseas were:

OFFICERS
    Lieutenant-Colonel T. P. Kidd, M.C.
    Major J. M. Forster, M.C.
    Major W. H. M. Lane, M.C.
    Major P. G. Hunt.
    Major R. H. Daljit Singh.
    Major B. J. Sutton.
    Major D. S. MacDonald.
    Captain E. K. Janjua.
    Captain H. M. Zia.
    Captain Hamid Khan.
    Captain H. H. Marsden.
    Captain T. M. Creasy.
    Captain R. J. W. Craig, M.C.
    Lieutenant Hamid-Ur-Rehman.

Lieutenant W. C. Moncrieff.
Lieutenant Mohd Anwar Khan.
Lieutenant P. R. Archer.

VICEROY'S COMMISSIONED OFFICERS

Subadar-Major Shahra Khan.
Subadar Bostan Khan.
Subadar Abdul Wahab.
Subadar Mohd Khan I.
Subadar Walait Ram.
Subadar Ismail Khan.
Subadar Gulistan Khan.
Subadar Jamna Dass.
Subadar Mohd Khan II.
Subadar Zaristan.
Subadar Sher Mohd.
Jemadar Rattan Chand.
Jemadar Sher Aslam.
Jemadar Sakhi Mohd, M.C.
Jemadar Ghulam Hussain.
Jemadar Amir Bahadur.
Jemadar Mohd Feroze.
Jemadar Tuab Gul.
Jemadar Parma Nand.
Jemadar Mohd Khan III.
Jemadar Nanak Chand.
Jemadar Dost Mohd.
Jemadar Nur Hussain.
Jemadar Sada Nand.

The following non-commissioned officers and men served with the Battalion throughout its overseas service:

15716 Havildar Khan Bahadur.
6899 Havildar Hakim Khan.
16260 Havildar-Clerk Bashir Ahmed.
20779 Lance-Havildar Sultan Mubarik.
17195 Lance-Havildar Ghulam Hussain.
16104 Sepoy Feroze Khan.
20934 Sepoy Adalat Khan.
20526 Sepoy Ghulam Haider.
3230969 Sepoy Din Dar.

Those whose names are printed in italics had served with the Battalion since it left India in July, 1941, and deserve, perhaps more than anyone else, the title which has been chosen for this History—"Capital Campaigners."

The number of campaign stars and war medals awarded to the Battalion for the Second World War is as follows:

1939-45 Star	900
Africa Star, with Eighth Army Clasp	900
Italy Star	900
War Medal	500
Overseas Defence Medal	200
India Service Medal	25

In addition, thirty-six *Jangi Inams* were granted for outstanding war service by the Government of India.

APPENDIX I

LIST OF COMMANDING OFFICERS

FIRST BELOOCH BATTALION—3RD BN. 10TH BALUCH REGT.

Name	Date of Appointment From	To
Bt.-Major J. Jackson	May 1844	May 1853
Lt.-Colonel R. Farquhar	May 1853	Oct. 1860
Capt. H. Beville	Oct. 1860	Dec. 1880
Lt.-Colonel T. Bell	Dec. 1880	Dec. 1885
Lt.-Colonel G. C. Sartorious, C.B.	Dec. 1885	Dec. 1892
Major W. A. Broome (p.s.)	Dec. 1892	Dec. 1899
Major (temp. Lt.-Colonel) G. E. Even	Dec. 1899	Jan. 1907
Lt.-Colonel F. J. Fowler, D.S.O.	Jan. 1907	Aug. 1913
Lt.-Colonel C. O. O. Tanner	Aug. 1913	Aug. 1918
Lt.-Colonel H. Hulseberg, D.S.O.	Aug. 1918	Dec. 1919
Lt.-Colonel A. E. Stewart, M.C.	Jan. 1920	July 1927
Lt.-Colonel A. S. Auret, O.B.E.	July 1927	May 1931
Lt.-Colonel M. L. A. Gompertz (p.s.c.)	May 1931	Jan. 1934
Lt.-Colonel J. F. Meiklejohn (p.s.c.)	Jan. 1934	Jan. 1938
Lt.-Colonel J. S. Harvey	Jan. 1938	Jan. 1941
Lt.-Colonel J. R. James (p.s.c.)	Jan. 1941	May 1941
Lt.-Colonel A. C. Taylor, D.S.O.	May 1941	May 1944
Lt.-Colonel L. V. S. Sherwood, D.S.O.	May 1944	Sept. 1945
Lt.-Colonel T. P. Kidd, M.C.	Sept. 1945	Feb. 1946

APPENDIX II

BIBLIOGRAPHY

CHAPTER ONE
1. "Life of Sir Charles Napier," Vol. III, 77.
2. 24th April, 1848, in Sind Govt. Records.
3. No. 2153 of 20th March, 1851, Sind Govt. Records.

CHAPTER TWO
1. No. 149 of 20th March, 1856, Sind Govt. Records.
2. Pelly's "Views and Opinions of General Jacob," p. 371 *et seq.*
3. Maude's "Oriental Campaigns," p. 162.
4. Frere's "Life," p. 182.
5. Gray's Diary, *Journal Soc. A.H.R.*, X, No. 39.
6. *Ibid.*, No. 39a.
7. Keith Young: "Siege of Delhi," p. 269.
8. Roberts: "Forty-one Years in India," I, p. 239.
9. *Ibid.*, p. 287.
   Forrest: I, pp. 142-43.
10. Malleson: II, p. 287.
11. Forrest: III, p. 387.
    Russell's Diary in India, II, p. 29.
12. "Views and Opinions of General Jacob," p. 168.
13. Secretary of State's Letters, No. 406, 30th November, 1863.

CHAPTER THREE
1. Fortescue: Vol. XIII, p. 471.
2. Official History, p. 598.

CHAPTER FOUR
1. Govt. of India, Military Dept., No. 482 of 1st May, 1896.
2. Army Order No. 24 of 28th September, 1894

CHAPTER FIVE
War Office, Army Order No. 29 of 1st February, 1911.

*

NOTE.—The sources of information used to compile this History are varied, most of them documentary, some hearsay, and a few personal, but all—within the limits of human fallibility—as accurate as circumstances and time permit. The History would never have been written in its present form if the author had not been given the invaluable draft of the first seven chapters written by the eminent historian of the Bombay Army, Sir Patrick Cadell, C.S.I., C.I.E. This draft was prepared before the Second World War, and, except for a few alterations and additions, remains much the same as written by him.

The first five chapters have been annotated numerically (above) to show the historical documentation of the various authorities consulted. For the period 1918 to 1939 the Battalion quarterly News-Letter and the Proceedings of the Karachi Annual Conferences are the most important sources. As this period coincided largely with the writer's service in the Battalion the events portrayed are written as objectively as possible.

Chapters Nine, Ten, Eleven and Twelve, which deal with the Second World War—a mere six years of a hundred years' history—occupy too many pages proportionately. Equally worthy space could have been devoted to the Afghan War, to Magdala, to the astonishing Uganda Campaign, but unfortunately day-to-day details of the Battalion's experiences in these wars are not available, nor have we any information of daily life and training in Sind cantonments during Queen Victoria's reign.

On the other hand, the events of the Second World War are fresh in memory The loss at Mersa Matruh of the War Diaries was partly compensated for by the timely publication of a short War History describing events up to and including the invasion of Sicily. The campaigns in Persia, the Desert, Italy and Greece are described from this book, the subsequent War Diaries, and from the following publications:

"African Trilogy." Alan Moorehead. (Hamish Hamilton.)
"Middle East, 1940-1942." Philip Guedalla. (Hodder & Stoughton.)
The Daily Telegraph "Story of the War," 1943. (Hodder & Stoughton.)
"The Tiger Kills," 1944. (H.M. Stationery Office.)
"The Tiger Triumphs," 1946. (*Ibid.*)

The author is furthermore indebted to many officers, past and present, of the 3rd Baluch who have sent him notes, or checked the manuscript. Among them are Colonels P. R. Quayle, J. R. James, A. C. Taylor and D. Carroll. Majors M. Forster and W. H. M. Lane gave considerable help in the last four chapters. Finally, to the Colonel of the Battalion, Colonel A. E. Stewart, M.C., who has read every line and has made numerous suggestions and improvements, the author's most grateful thanks are due.

W. E. M.

INDEX

A
Abdul Ghani, Mess Abdar, 83.
Abyssinia, 25 *et seq*.
Ahwaz, 102.
Alamein, El, 104, 113, 120 *et seq*.
Arogi, 26.
Athens, 147.
Auchinleck, Field-Marshal Sir Claude, 104, 106, 116, 152.

B
Baluchis, Enlistment of, (q.v., Organization), 45, 75.
Baluch Regiment, other battalions:
    1st Battalion, 23, 35, 37, 53, 68, 81, 103.
    2nd Battalion, 35, 40, 42, 53.
    4th Battalion, 7, 9, 13, 22, 24, 28, 30, 31, 33, 34, 56, 62, 91, 103, 107, 138, 144.
    5th Battalion, 24, 29, 34, 40, 43, 60.
Band, 80, 82.
Bandar Shahpur, 96.
Battalion, Training, 72.
Benghazi, 122.
Burma, 32, 83 *et seq*.
Bushire, 14, 70, 99.

C
Campaigns:
    Mutiny, 15 *et seq*.; Abyssinia, 25 *et seq*.; Second Afghan War, 28 *et seq*.; Burma, 32 *et seq*.; Uganda, 36 *et seq*.; East Africa, 59 *et seq*.; Persia, 68 *et seq*.; Burma, 83 *et seq*.; Western Desert, 104 *et seq*.; El Alamein, 120 *et seq*.; Sicily, 124 *et seq*.; Italy, 132-134; Greece, 146 *et seq*.
Casualties, 17, 18, 38, 40, 41, 57, 66, 113, 118, 124, 138, 142, 144, 148.
Centenary, 135.
Chagherzais, 44.
Chetwode, Field-Marshal Sir Philip, 86.
Chikor, 5.
Colours, 24, 45.
Composition (q.v. Enlistment Areas).
Cross, Christian, Magdala, 27.

D
Deir el Shein, 117, 119.
Delhi, 16.
Dogra Brahmans, 75.
Dress, 3, 4, 5, 9, 10, 22, 33, 47, 48, 82.
Drill, 4, 49, 156.
Durand Line, 34.

E
Enlistment Areas (q.v. Organization), 4, 8, 32, 75, 87.

F
Fortescue, 28.
Fourth Indian Division, 105, 120, 134, 138, 141, 143, 144, 147, 148.

G
Gemmano Ridge, 143.
Gothic Line, 138, 142.

H
Haft Khel, 100.
Honours, Battle, 14, 23, 24, 28, 31, 40, 41, 57, 71.
Hurs, 34.

J
Jacob, John, 1, 8, 11, 14.
Jacob, Field-Marshal Sir Claud, 35, 72.

K
Kandahar, 30.
Karens, 32.
Kidney Ridge, 121.
Kitchener Test, 43.
Kot Abdullah, 102.
Kurram Shahr, 101.

L
Light Infantry, Designation as, 27.

M
Macedonia, 149.
Magdala, 27.
Mahsuds, 44, 53, 57, 58.
Maiwand, 29.

Medals:
  First World War, 71.
  Second World War, 159.
Mekran, 34, 41.
Mersa Matruh, 104, 109 et seq.
Mess, Officers', 51, 87, 133.
Messina, 132.
Mian Gul, Naik, 112.
Mir Badshah, Mahsud, 44.
Montgomery, General, 121, 122, 128.
Mounted Infantry, 32, 52, 84.
Mussolini, 116, 130.
Mutiny, 1857, 15 et seq.

N

Napier, Sir Charles, 1, 2, 3, 5.
Napier, Sir Robert, 25, 27.

O

Officers:
  Auret, A. S., 52, 73, 78, 79, 80, 82.
  Bannerman, 16, 17.
  Beville, H., 10, 16, 25, 27.
  Broome, W. A., 37.
  Brown, R. H., 98, 122, 136.
  Chatterji, 110, 116.
  Craig, R. J. W., 135, 143, 151.
  Crimmin, J., V.C., 33.
  Daljit Singh R. H., 136.
  Dalton, D. F., 84, 87, 134.
  Davies, R. D., 50, 56, 82.
  Even, E. G., 43, 45.
  Farquhar, R., 10, 15, 18, 20.
  Forster, J. M., 93, 100, 110, 119, 135, 138, 149, 153, 157.
  Fowler, F. J., 37, 39, 40, 43, 48, 49, 50, 77.
  Frey, 110.
  Gompertz, M. L. A., 79, 81, 82 et seq.
  Grant, J., 31.
  Hamid Khan, A., 99, 110, 117, 137.
  Hannyngton, J. A., 37, 38.
  Harvey, J. S., 68, 73, 88.
  Hickenbotham, 137.
  Hicks, J. (Pasha), 16.
  Hulseberg, H., 63, 68.
  Humphreys, G. G. P., 56, 57.
  Jackson, B., 136, 152.
  Jackson, J., 6.
  Jackson, P. E., 152, 156.
  James, J. R., 68, 73, 90, 93.
  Kidd, T. P., 138, 140, 157.
  Lake, E. A. W., 51, 52, 63, 68, 82.
  Lane, W. H. M., 117, 140, 143, 149.
  McCudden, 52.
  Maxwell, W. E., 93, 96, 102, 136.
  Maxwell, W. L., 52, 58.
  Mayor, G., 6, 10.
  Meiklejohn, J. F., 82, 86.
  Merriman, 59, 63.
  Moriarty, G. O'N., 84.
  Nailor, K. J. F., 154.
  Price, C. V. H., 37, 39, 40.
  Quayle, P., 50, 82.
  Robinson, J. F., 102, 109.
  Sardar Ali, 116, 140, 142.
  Sartorius, G. C., 32.
  Sherwood, L. V. S., 135 et seq., 150, 153.
  Sime, A. W. H., 83, 87.
  Southey, W. M., 37, 38.
  Stewart, A. E., 73 et seq.
  Tanner, C. O. O., 37, 40, 44, 59, 64.
  Tate, J. C., 42, 59, 86.
  Taylor, A. C., 73, 78, 88, 93 et seq., 110, 114, 133, 135.
  Tighe, M., 32, 37, 39, 40, 41.
  Van Loo, G., 96, 115.
  Vokes, J. M., 101.
  Vora, D. N., 132.
  Waller, R. C. B., 85.
  Wetherall, F. B. G., 76.
  Wright, 6.
Organization, 31, 33, 35, 43, 66, 72, 75, 80, 93, 125, 131.

P

Palestine, 103, 106.
Pay, 4, 51.
Persia, 14, 68 et seq., 96 et seq.
Polo, 51.
Poona, 46 et seq.
Punjabi Musulmans, 87.

Q

Queen Mary, Her Majesty, 6, 45, 73, 75, 77, 135.
Queen Mary's Own, title, 45.

R

Raising, 1st Belooch, 2.
Rations, 47.
Razmak, 88.
Recruiting (q.v. Enlistment Areas).
Reports, General Inspection, 8, 9, 11, 14, 17, 22, 34, 45, 53, 86, 117, 123, 128, 142.
Roberts, Field-Marshal Sir Frederick, 30.
Rommel, 104, 106.
Russia, 14, 56.
Ruweisat Ridge, 115 et seq.

S

San Marino, 143.
Scobie, General, 156.
Secunderabad, 83.
Shiraz, 70.

Sicily, 129 *et seq.*
Smuts, 60, 61.
Somaliland, 45.
Strength, 7, 21, 23, 32, 58, 59, 138, 153.
Subedar-Majors:
    Samueljee Israel, 27, 31.
    Mir Badshah, 44.
    Yar Muhammad, 45.
    Ahmed Khan, 84, 87.
    Ahmed Nur, 95.
    Nasib Khan, 132.
    Akbar Khan, 133, 153.
    Shahra Khan, 156, 157.
Syracuse, 131.

T

Tenth Indian Division, 108, 109, 110, 120.
Tobruk, 104, 122.

U

UNRRA, 156.
Urbino, 141.

V

Veroia, 150, 157.
Victoria Cross, 33, 57.
Volos, 148.

W

Wana, 81.
White, Field-Marshal Sir George, 33.

Y

Yusuf Khan, Naik, 38.

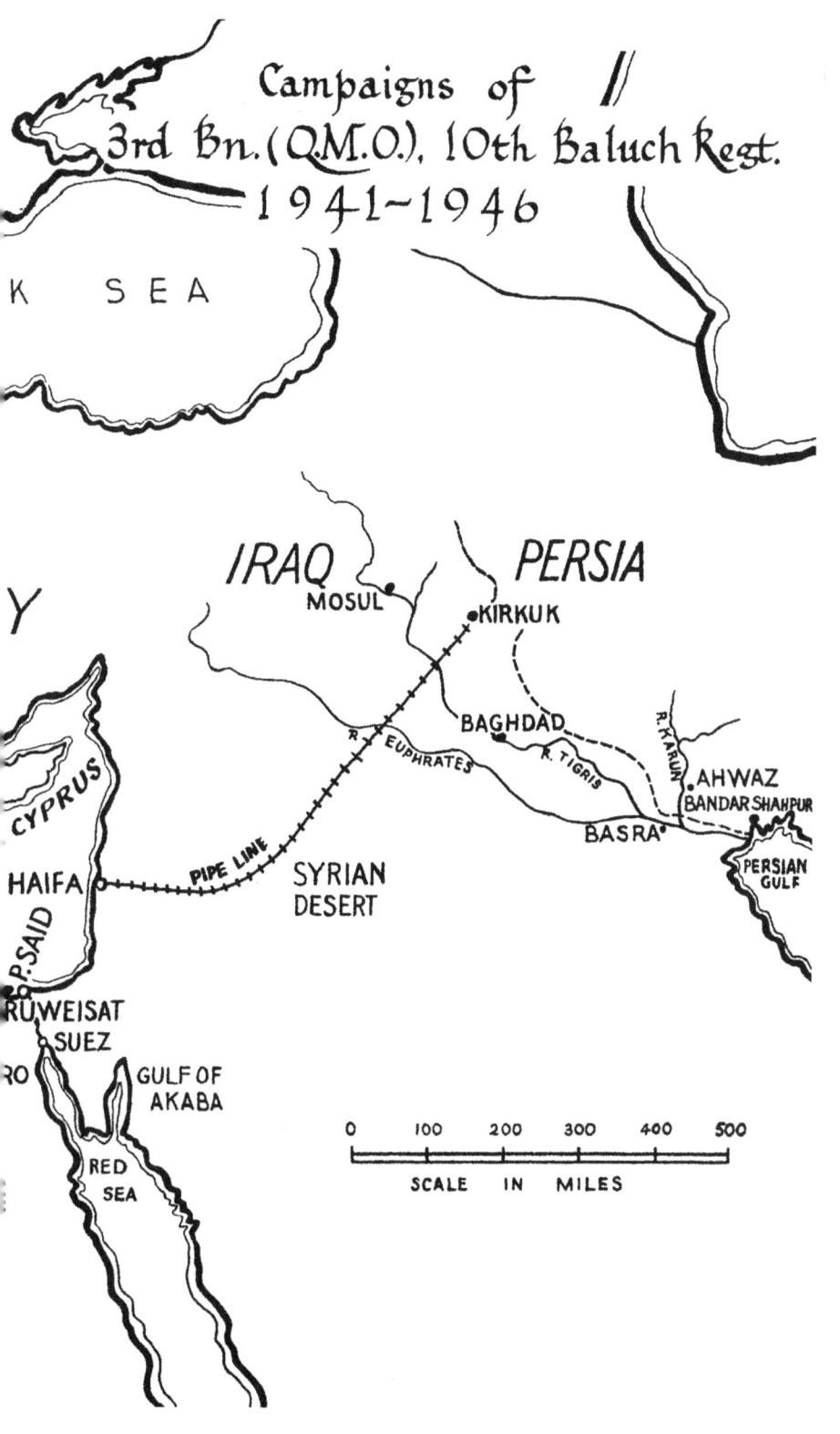

www.ingramcontent.com/pod-product-compliance
Lightning Source LLC
Chambersburg PA
CBHW031144160426
43193CB00008B/252